Mom

Happy Christmas

John

CORNWALL
— *Seasons* —

ROY PHILLIPS

HALSGROVE

First published in Great Britain in 2002

DEDICATION
Rak Liz Tregenza Gans Karenza

British Library Cataloguing-in-Publication Data
A CIP record for this title is available from the British Library

ISBN 1 84114 191 7
Catalogue data is available from the British Library

HALSGROVE
Halsgrove House
Lower Moor Way
Tiverton, Devon EX16 6SS
Tel: 01884 243242
Fax: 01884 243325
email sales@halsgrove.com
website www.halsgrove.com

Printed and bound by D'Auria Industrie Grafiche Spa, Italy

CONTENTS

The area covered by this book is mainly to the west of the River Fal, although most of the observations apply to the whole of Cornwall. Pictured is the Lizard from Kynance, where wild flowers proliferate and seabirds nest along the cliffs and on Mullion Island.

CORNWALL

Padstow •

• Newquay

• Liskeard

• St Agnes

• St Austell

St Ives
Bay
St Ives •
Zennor •   • Hayle
Pendeen •
St Just •   Penzance
           •   • Marazion
Sennen •   • Porthleven

Mount's
Bay

Land's End

• Lizard

Lizard Point

PREFACE

The call of the wild appeals to us all. Whether it be to explore remote regions of the earth, visit our own countryside, grow a geranium or keep a few fishes in a tank, there is a universal appreciation of the wonders around us. Wildlife has been my own abiding interest, thanks to being hopeless at sport. When the two toughest boys of the class were singled out to choose two teams, I was always the last to be picked. Having been finally and reluctantly chosen, I would be relegated to some far-flung corner of the field where decisive play was unlikely. Here, I was free to daydream and watch the fluttering butterflies, the opening daisies and swallows catching midges over the pitch. I have been watching them ever since.

Cornwall has been the ancestral home of my family for a long time. Six generations of them have lived in the same street. The men have been fishermen, horsemen, seamen, miners or tradesmen, adapting to whatever the economic climate required, even acquiring formal education if they had to. The women supported them in all their endeavours and, as was the way of things, were often the quiet strength that succoured both man and child through the vagaries of fortune. As a result I nurture that deep love of Cornwall that only those who have such ancient affinities with their homeland can appreciate. By way of the pages in this book I hope to share that love with my fellow Cornishmen* and all others, both residents and visitors, who also have an affection for this land and its wildlife.

*I use the term Cornish*men* and *man*kind in the old-fashioned way, to include men, women and children, dead or alive, and as yet unborn.

Roy Phillips

FOREWORD

It is a rare privilege to be asked to write a foreword of a new publication especially if the book is written by a friend, and one so devoted to the wildlife of Cornwall.

I first met Roy Phillips (NRP) in the early 1950s when I had recently settled in the West Penwith area. I remember clearly that he was sitting astride the wall on the Hayle estuary causeway, dressed in faded blue jeans and wearing a hooded camouflage jacket, and was eagerly watching the wading birds on the estuary as the tide gently moved them towards his position.

We introduced ourselves and during our chat he told me of the exciting seabird migration off the Island of St Ives during north-westerly gales. I jumped at the opportunity that autumn to join him and a friend, Philip Pearce, in what I can only describe as a magical seabird migration watch. Many hundreds of gannets, shearwaters, kittiwakes and auks, plus the occasional skua and petrel battled against a westerly gale and passed the Island where we sheltered. I returned home that evening having been taught a lot about seabirds and longing for the next gale, of which there were to be many in the years to follow.

That was the start of our long friendship – early-morning walks along the coast, bird-watching and looking at other wildlife, provided that Philip and I could get Roy out of bed on time! He taught me many things: of 'dark easterlies', winds and tides, sunfish and St Ives people. It is also worth a mention that it was due to Roy's far-sightedness and enthusiasm that seabird migration studies from St Ives, and the small valleys such as Porthgwarra, near Land's End, became a magnet for so many bird-watchers from all over Britain in the spring and autumn.

This book, his third main publication, brings together the results of his tireless observations, reflecting his love of the Cornish countryside.

Robin Khan MBE, 2002

ACKNOWLEDGEMENTS

Certain sections of the following appeared as articles in various publications, mainly the *St Ives Times & Echo*, *BBC Wildlife Magazine*, *Ydhyn yn Kernow* and other publications of the CBWPS. The verses are quoted from *The Book of a Thousand Poems* published by Evans Bros, London 1942. The author has tried unsuccessfully to determine copyright of Adeline White and C.M. Lowe. Special thanks, also, to Liz Gynn for help with the manuscript and botany. Like everyone who enjoys the countryside, I am indebted to those conservation societies who have done so much to preserve our precious landscape and its wildlife, including the National Trust, Cornwall Wildlife Trust, the Cornwall Bird Watching and Preservation Society, and the Royal Society for the Protection of Birds. We are also indebted to the many private landowners and farmers who care for the countryside and allow the public the privilege of sharing the wildlife on their property. Many thanks to them all.

Trevaylor stream in winter. In such a narrow peninsula, with a small catchment area, large rivers and streams are inevitably few. Where undisturbed they hold pairs of dippers, grey wagtails, and otters.

In springtime the cliffs are awash with colour, sea campion and thrift blending in a dazzling display.

PREAMBLE

As an infant at school in St Ives, my class was taken out to see an aeroplane. It must have been just before the Second World War. We climbed to the top of the Trenwith Burrows and stood on the spoil from the abandoned mine, and waited for it to fly over. I can't remember what kind of plane it was, a single-seater as I recall, red, and we were told it had won the Schneider Trophy, whatever that was.

As we waited for the historic moment I could see, beyond the cottage roofs yellow with lichen, the green waters of the bay where my grandfather was out sailing his skiff. After school, or on Saturdays, he would take me out and show me, down on the surface, the real world in which I lived. I was not interested in aeroplanes, whereas the love of natural things has always been with me.

In those distant summer days, as the skiff tacked across the bay, my grandfather, who would never have been so presumptuous as to call himself a naturalist, used to sail close to the basking sharks and porpoises as he pointed out the passing birds. They flew alongside the boat, low over the water or, in the case of the gannets, soared high overhead, circling, until their dives guided us to the fish and we cast our spinners overboard.

'Over there,' he said, 'kiddas look!'

Scores of them were flying back to the cliffs at Godrevy and Hell's Mouth where their mates lined up on ledges with a solitary egg tucked between their legs. Much later, I found them in the bird books under the name of guillemot, and then, as my knowledge progressed, *Uria aalge*. We Cornish have sacrificed much in adapting to a changing age, especially in our speech, but those birds are still kiddas in the memory of those distant days. Skimming packs of passing mackerel-birds fell under our stern; even for him, the Cornish name of skidden for these Manx shearwaters was long forgotten. Then, on the water, we might see the pied plumage of a pope, with its coloured bill full of dripping lances.

Pendeen from Levant Mine. An early autumn scene with the heather in full bloom, looking east from Levant Mine to Pendeen. Old abandoned industrial sites are now an important feature of wild Cornwall and hold many interesting species.

And, 'There,' he would say as the terns flew by, 'mirrets!'

Morwhennol they were in Cornish, sea swallows, skimming by in little flocks, graceful and white, plunging from the sky with excited calls. Sometimes, although I never heard my grandfather name them such, the Cornish called them scarraweet which must surely be onomatopoeic, from the call of the migrating sandwich terns as they keep in contact with their dependent young. Keer-ik, is how it is transcribed today, which doesn't catch the nature the call anything like as well.

Basking sharks were seen every summer. They came, like gentle giants, nosing into the shallows on warm, calm days, and we could sail so close that we could see their white lips, lapping the plankton, and a flick of the massive tails could have capsized our little skiff and thrown us into the sea. My grandfather laughed at my fear. 'They wain't hurt 'ee.' But I knew the damage they could do to nets, and our little boat seemed so frail beside these monsters. Porpoises were common then. We saw them frequently and sometimes, though these were always rare in the bay, we might see dolphins leaping in the distance. Once, and what a memory, there were so many fish in the bay that the sea was alive with them. They came into the bay in thousands. No, millions! There was one vast shoal of sprat, driven to pass close inshore by I-know-not-what, on that one occasion and never since in all my years, and all the predators of the sea were after them.

Outside the sprat were shoals of mackerel, driving them closer to the shore. The mackerel drove the sprat into the harbour and they came in a shoal so tight that, in the corner by the lifeboat-house, they were packed in a solid silver mass a foot above the surface as more and more fish were driven under them by the predatory mackerel, until the sprat were forced up to die, as if on dry land, by the sheer thrust of fish beneath them. Outside the harbour, as gannets plunged in a gluttonous feast, a rolling school of porpoises in a feeding-frenzy marshalled the mackerel in turn, driving them in until they too were packing the harbour. Then we caught them by foul-hooking as others scooped the sprat up in buckets for toasting, and a few for the cat.

There was no sale for such sudden vast numbers of fish, no freezers, no cannery or smoking-houses here then. I have never seen so many living creatures together in one place, one body, like a massive corporate identity of life, the product of a bounteous ocean which provided sustenance for an unseen myriad of creatures within its unpolluted depths. It was living evidence of the sheer profusion of nature and they were left un-netted for the survivors to continue on their way. Shall we ever see such sights again? Nowadays, every last one would be caught, frozen, pulverised for manure, dried to fuel a power station, or even dumped back into the sea to rot if the boats are over quota.

In the wartime winters came the herring shoals. When I went to the pier-head at dusk to wave my father off into the blacked-out night we saw the dim shapes of herring birds, great northern divers, all the way from Greenland and Canada, which fed not on the herring but hunted for the green shore-crabs along the rocky coast and among the wrack in the harbour. And once, when a great northern diver became entangled on abandoned fishing gear, I brought it into our old pilchard cellar to remove the line and hook. There, in that dark enclosure where it could see neither sea nor sky the bird uttered the most haunting and plaintive wail that I have ever heard among all the sounds of nature. It was a cry of despair and a yearning for that which was lost to it... the sea, the sky, freedom. It was the cry of the loon. When I later heard them

The uniform greens of summer create a tranquil scene along the north-coast path.

Pendeen from the east. Viewed from Bosigran on such a calm day, it is hard to envisage the storms that blow thousands of seabirds close to shore.

calling to their young on a Canadian lake I was reminded of that bird wintering in our Cornish bay. After freeing it of the hook and line I laid it with reverence in the shallow water and watched it glide away, with just one backward glance, as if in gratitude.

To the woods, the moors and valleys, I went alone in those childhood days for, as far as I am aware, my grandfather was never seen more than a hundred yards or so inland from the shore if he could help it. I listened to the buzzing insects on the marshes and watched the water-rats become encrusted with living silver, like the fish in the sea, as their fur carried a coating of air beneath the surface of the meandering stream at Hellesveor. And there were cirl buntings among the elm trees by the Ludgvan farms, woodlarks composing melodies along the boundaries of meadows at St Erth, and corncrakes and quail calling from the hayfields on the Lizard.

Those days are over. The porpoises, puffins and herrings have almost gone from these waters, as have woodlarks and yellowhammers from the land. Hundreds of acres of moorland have been broken in for agriculture. Water-rats are almost extinct. There is less of everything alive, apart from humans, although more is recorded and photographed and filmed. The annual reports of natural history societies report more sightings of creatures and rare birds than ever before as we desperately search for all that is lost and become ornithologists, lepidopterists, lichenologists; experts in narrow fields. One lost bird can draw a crowd of thousands.

However, while things are not entirely satisfactory in the wildwood, they are not altogether lost and progress is being made. Thirty years ago, after I had given a talk on the birds of Afghanistan and Kashmir, I was asked, 'What does it matter if a few species do die out?' I could find no answer that would satisfy the questioner, for he had never looked at the world through my eyes. For him, I had to concede, it mattered not a jot, for he was unaware of the riches around him, whereas I regarded all living species as jewels too precious to lose and hoarded them like a miser. After many years of gloom and despondency as the wild things around us suffered and diminished to, and sometimes past, the point of extinction, we now see a rising determination to cherish our natural heritage that is influencing the future development of the world. We are coming to realise that mother nature is a generous parent, asking for herself only the so-called wastelands, the bogs and stony ground of little economic importance, in which our falling seeds will not flourish anyway. In Cornwall, there has never been a more optimistic time for wildlife in my memory, for we have at last a public awareness of what we can do, either for good or bad, with more members of conservation societies than all the political parties put together. There would be few today who would ask, 'What does it matter?'

Cornwall is a small part of a small kingdom in a big wide world. It has no mighty rivers, no high mountains, no deep forests, no huge lakes, swamps, sweltering deserts or icy wastes. We do, however, have meandering streams, moorland, small woods, reservoirs, marshes, sand dunes, agriculture, gardens, beaches, estuaries and, influencing all, the sea. Such a wide variety, in such a small area, is precisely what makes it so diverse and interesting in its wildlife. We are aware of great natural features throughout the world and see their images on our television screens in startling detail. At times it seems that we know more of these remote regions than we do of the wildlife on our doorstep or in the back garden, but there is much to see in our little corner.

This natural arch in the rocks at Roscommon Cliff is encrusted in black Verrucaria maura *lichen. It is near Stamps an Jowl Zawn (The stamps of the Devil), a proper bit of Kernewek surviving in a place name. Zawn, for a deep cleft in a cliff, is a Cornish language word adopted by climbers, for there is no English equivalent. Such flat areas of rock are used by both gulls and shags as resting places.*

It is essential to appreciate that little of Cornwall is natural. Ancient forests were felled for agriculture, the timber used for ships and mines, the granite taken from the carns and cliffs for monuments and buildings. All of it has been modified in some way by man over the centuries, with the exception perhaps of the very narrow band of land from the cliff tops to the sea. Even here, sheep and goats were grazed until fairly recently, and the wounds of mining still scar the headlands and valley mouths with adits and spoil. But mother nature, ever patiently waiting, eventually reclaims her own. Mine stacks crumble, trees grow in the stennacks (where tin mining took place), bracken invades abandoned land, brambles flourish. Left to herself nature would eventually clothe the whole landscape in forest and scrub, as it was in primeval times.

A typical community of bog plants, with mosses, cross-leaved heath and sundews.

That wild things were more abundant in the past is certain. In our youth we took this abundance for granted, as we did the wild areas that sustained it, for there was so much less pressure for development. We have lost a great deal, but we have also retained much and it is this remnant that I would like to enjoy with you. By illustrating a few Cornish subjects through the four seasons, I hope to share reminiscences and a personal view of a landscape that has sustained and inspired me for a lifetime. It is not intended for this little book to be a treatise on the identification or the distribution of species, for there are many such excellent guides available. Neither shall it be a stuffy tome of facts and figures, or to imply that specialists' knowledge is a prerequisite for the enjoyment of nature. My intention is to further your interest in our countryside by indicating just what might be seen and when to look for it, in the hope that you too may go out and be soaked by rain, stung by bees, chased by bulls, get bitten by midges, fall in mud and arrive home late for supper... in pursuit of a lifetime's enjoyment.

Finding this wellie boot while looking for bog plants raised a good laugh, but it was a long hop home for somebody.

While enjoying nature, we should remember that we are but passers-by, ephemeral in the millennia, yet, like the ravens in the Tower, we are also custodians of the past, guardians of the future and observers of the present. So, with a few diversions, let us wander through the seasons, investigate what they offer and see what we can find.

Members of the Cornwall Wildlife Trust visit Pendarves Wood nature reserve in May to see the rich carpet of bluebells.

GWAYNTEN

SPRING

Look! look! the spring is come
O feel the gentle air,
That wanders thro' the boughs to burst
The thick buds everywhere!

First spring morning Robert Bridges

The young year, bursting with barely constrained enthusiasm for life, with lengthening days and swelling buds, might be a time to reflect on our own young days and the influences that made us what we are. Like, I suspect, many another brought up in Cornwall, the first wild thing I ever knew the name of, and my first recognisable word, so my grandmother told me, was gull. Well, 'gulla', in fact, but that was near enough for an embryonic ornithologist, and I didn't know it was a Cornish dialect word at the time. I was introduced to proper bird-watching by a school friend's father. He took us out to Clodgy (St Ives) to watch the yellowhammers, linnets and stonechats building nests among the gorse. Maybe there was an ulterior motive, in that he wanted linnets' and goldfinches' eggs to put under his canaries but, with no binoculars or books, we learned fieldcraft. We tracked down the birds from a distance, learning call-notes, observing the differing behaviour of males and females, nest-site preferences and clutch sizes. Very scientific! Later, in about 1942, I do remember buying a battered second-hand copy of Vere Benson's *Observer's Book of British Birds* from a school pal for two bob (shillings) saved from my pocket money. A new one would have been four bob and to earn such a sum would have required an inordinate amount of Saturday-morning errands to be run for my great aunts at a penny a time. I was shamed, but not surprised, to see that Vere Benson had founded the Bird Lovers' League following

Small pearl-bordered fritillary. A butterfly of dry heaths, it flies in May, thus being vulnerable to cold, wet springs. The larval food plant is wild violet, not at all uncommon in Cornwall.

cruelty she had witnessed in Cornwall. During the war many thousands of birds were oiled after the sinking of ships off our coast and, as a schoolchild in those coarse grey-flannel shorts, I got into a fight with some other local boys who were using oiled guillemots as targets for stone throwing. I have been in fights on behalf of conservation ever since but, at that time, guillemots, shags, seals and all birds of prey were fair game, or even subject to bounty, as was anything else deemed to compete with man. The abundance of birds meant that a few taken for cages or shot for sport made little difference to the overall population of most species. It is very different today.

Many years later Vere Benson gave me a signed copy of her book, and I believe no publication before or since did more to encourage the love and conservation of birds than that little volume. I still treasure it, and well remember the first birds that I identified using it: a purple sandpiper, then, around 1945, my first little egret at Hayle estuary, seen from the train on the way to school. Little egrets were very rare and the authorities at the time thought that it could not have been a genuine vagrant but possibly an escape from captivity. My optics comprised just one half of an old brass draw-tube binocular which came apart with an audible pop if pulled out too far, so maybe I was mistaken. Perhaps it was a white paper bag but, in true twitching practice, I ticked it anyway. Little egrets have since expanded their range and are now commonly found here in winter and are known to be breeding in the county. Eventually I acquired a proper pair of 'bins', which were nothing like as good as the optics available now, and went forth with the *Observer's Book* and all hung about with my 8-by-25s and clothed in ex-service camouflage gear complete with used footwear marked *'Boots, Don R. Other Ranks, for the use of'* from the Army & Navy Stores, and guaranteed *'Fair wear or another pair'*.

Hart's-tongue fern. Flourishing in shady woods and banks, along with several other ferns, the hart's-tongue is semi-evergreen but at its best when fresh new growth unfolds in spring.

In 1951, in W.H. Smith's in Truro I saw a copy of Witherby's *Handbook of British Birds*, five volumes for £7. My wages were about a fiver a week, but here were birds and knowledge upon which dreams and life-lists were made. All else was abandoned: no cigarettes, no beer, no girls, in order to save for that book. It was the ultimate in ornithological literature at a time when books were beginning to appear on all aspects of natural history and laying the foundations of the wide interest now evident. Since then, with improved printing techniques and a huge potential market, many new field guides of superb quality and accuracy have appeared, and I have a library of natural history books, yet still find myself referring to the old, battered *Handbook* as the most concise and readable of them all. However, nothing, absolutely nothing, including all the reference books ever published, can supplant actually going out and seeing things for yourself.

So, to springtime! When does it begin? We can usually define summer as June, July and August with some certainty. It follows that September, October and November are autumn and therefore December, January and February are winter, leaving March April and May as the months of spring. That may be the logical approach and we know when we see the recognised signs of spring but, in our mild maritime climate, the calendar is of little value in arranging a date to greet it. Frog-spawn can appear in December (2002), celandines in February,

The spring sunshine emerges from behind the clouds of winter. Look to the skies now for displaying buzzards and ravens.

migrant birds in March, the first cuckoo in April, while the last of the swifts do not arrive until late May or even into June. In some years the touch of winter is so light that the change in seasons is barely perceptible. Enthusiastic daffodils thrust through frozen soil in December, even November if conditions mean their biological clock is running fast. The gorse appraises the season by opening a few tentative blooms throughout the winter, before risking its full flush of gold, for in exceptional years the snows and cold easterlies persist until after the Easter eggs have all been eaten.

The traditional heralds of spring are anticipated annually by most of us and everyone has their favourite harbinger of warm weather and opening blossoms. At sea level, the adult lesser black-backed gulls begin moving north in February and may be seen in flocks of a thousand or more, resting on our estuaries or the sandbanks at the mouths of harbours at low tide. The young go to Spain and North Africa, where most stay until they mature, while the adults are fairly short-distance migrants, coming from Scandinavia and Iceland to winter around the North Atlantic. In mild winters it seems hardly worth the effort for such a short stay away from the breeding grounds.

South-east winds in spring can bring many exotic species to beyond their normal range. A party of bee-eaters came to Kelynack, St Just, in May 2001. They are almost annual in Cornwall.

The lesser celandine is also an early sign of spring, its glistening golden petals reflecting the low sunshine in the shadows of roadside and ditch, as well as in the filtered light of bare-branched woodland. Around mid-March the first migrant passerine birds arrive. Out on the exposed headlands or high moors, where the living at this time of year is anything but easy, look for the species that for me is the truest herald of the beginning of spring. Perched on some prominent feature, a rock or fencepost, the first wheatears pause, totally motionless as a ploy to remain unnoticed, and then dip their bodies in rapid bows as they watch the approaching intruder. A quick flip and they are gone. Low over the ground they retreat, with their white rumps flashing, to peer at the interloper over the brow of the next prominence until it is safe to resume the search for the few insects available at this early date. I have known them to arrive on a high moor in a fine spell and begin the breeding cycle, only to be driven off again by a heavy fall of snow.

In very early spring, our resident birds are thinking of nesting. In March, ravens are already laying eggs, buzzards are well on the way to completing new nests, shags are busy settling on the cliffs and tearing out clumps of grass to line their seaweed nests, and peregrines are back on territory and visiting the potential eyrie.

Of all the birds to watch, none is more thrilling than the peregrine falcon. Its mastery of the air, whether in gale or calm, is unsurpassed, as is its fearlessness in tackling prey. Peregrines have been known to take birds ranging in size from herons to the tiny goldcrest, the former too heavy to carry and the latter hardly more than a morsel. Sadly, the first ones I saw were not on the wing but in a cage by the little pond at Hellesveor, St Ives, early in the Second World War. They were being taken from town to town and farm to farm to show the populace what they were and how to kill them. It was said that they were a threat to carrier pigeons bearing messages from aircraft that had ditched in the sea. That was utter bunkum but, such is the effect of propaganda, all our peregrines were wiped out in the interests of public morale.

As is well known, just as the recovery began, they were again wiped out by pesticides but, thankfully, they have now recovered from that disaster too. From a population of zero they have re-established themselves on a few of our cliffs, where every year a dedicated band of bird-watchers watches over them and monitors their progress. While having preferred sites for their eyries they are by no means faithful to any one ledge, and, as they build no nest, finding them can involve many hours of observation in early spring. As the young develop, the tell-tale 'whitewash' around the nest makes it more conspicuous but it is still remarkably difficult to find on a large cliff. One elusive pair was on territory for four years before I found the site. It was in an old shag's nest, so low down on a very low cliff, that it would have been considered totally unsuitable for a bird whose eyrie is supposed to be on a high ledge with panoramic views. I had not even thought of looking for it there, drenched by spray, although since then I have found a pair of ravens also occupying an ancient shag's ledge. Perhaps these ravens were driven from their own ancestral site by peregrines, for competition for the ideal ledge is fierce.

The best time to watch peregrines is when the young are learning the art of hunting prey. From hesitant first flight they develop into masters in a few weeks. They practise diving and turning by playing together in the air and by swooping on all manner of things to develop their prowess. You may enjoy watching them swoop on the drying heads of umbelliferous plants, snatching them off as they pass at speed. While learning fast, they are dependent on the parents until late in the autumn and the old birds teach them, step by step, to look after themselves. From delicately feeding the chicks with tiny pieces of meat they progress to dropping carcases at the eyrie and eventually bringing in

Amid the squalor of five weeks' occupation following a month's incubation of the eggs, these young peregrine falcons are almost ready to leave the eyrie. Their plumage is much duller than that of the adults, and the base of the bill, the cere, together with the skin around the eyes, is blue. Both will change to bright yellow as they mature.

prey for the young to snatch from their talons in flight. I once saw an adult bring in a pigeon and, just before the young one tried to snatch it, release the prey from its talons. The young pupil attempted to grab the falling bird but the pigeon, to the amazement of peregrines and watcher, recovered its wits, flew off at speed and escaped. I marvelled that a peregrine could catch a bird and bring it back uninjured for the young to pursue in training.

Another lucky survivor was a Manx shearwater snatched by a peregrine from over the sea. The load was just about as much as the predator could struggle back with to the cliff and, when dived on by a herring gull, it was forced to release the shearwater, which immediately dived below the surface and emerged some distance off before resuming its journey to South America. The peregrine came home empty-clawed. They are very fierce in defence of their eyries. A friend and I once saw a carrion crow that had pestered them to the limit grabbed in mid-air and taken to the nest site, out of our view. We thought that was the end of the crow, and a dinner for the peregrine chicks, but later it flapped out groggily from the site, no doubt having received a severe lesson. Another time I saw two peregrines beat up a whole family of ravens and eventually drive them to the ground where they hid under boulders until their tormentors had flown off. Nothing messes with a peregrine.

Before the leaves are fully open on deciduous trees, carpets of bluebells, the most spectacular of our native woodland flowers, may still be seen in the dappled sunshine of most of our woods. It is one of the plants said to be indicative of ancient forest; wood anemones are another. Where they occur is supposed to be where ancient forest has long been felled, leaving only the ground cover as a reminder of its previous existence. Maybe, but here both anemones and bluebells flourish in areas that probably never were wooded. The most impressive swathes of blue occur on the exposed cliffs and hillsides, where the wood anemone also thrives, the former doing best in the wetter sections and the latter preferring the dry upper slopes. In May, some damp, shaded cliffs are just a cascade of blue mist among the boulders, while the delicate anemones thrust through the dry mulch of accumulated bracken fronds. The anemones do not produce such an impressive burst of blossom, but their delicate petals, opening from March to June in some years, are among the most delightful of our wild flowers. Both anemones and bluebells thrive, in fact, in what are essentially woodland conditions, for the thick canopy of bracken fronds, which die off and fall in autumn, letting the winter sunlight reach to the ground, simulate the exact conditions found under deciduous trees. I say bluebells 'may still be seen' for they are under threat from the dreaded three-cornered leek, that alien white 'onion flower' that obliterates all in its relentless spread.

A quick look at the map will tell you that proper woodland is thin on the ground in Cornwall. An old saying states that 'if you show a Cornishman a tree, he will reach for an axe' (or is it an old saw?). In fairness, it must be remembered that Cornwall has not been forested for thousands of years and, in the recent past, there was no fuel other than that which grew here. Gorse and bracken were the fuels of the common people and extensively harvested, coal an expensive import. Timber was cut for ships and mines, with apparently very little replanting, and, apart from brushwood, was probably too precious to burn. All of which combined to create a barren landscape. Old photographs show just how bare it was: St Ives with no Tregenna Woods, Lamorna with not a tree in the whole valley, and not so long ago either, as photography is not an ancient art. So undoubtedly there are now more trees in Cornwall than for at least a few centuries, albeit that many of them are in plantations of conifer or self-sown tracts of sycamore. No matter, as long as the slower, but more persistent natives, such as oak, elm and beech, are also permitted to regenerate. Plantations of conifers, as on the Lizard and to a lesser extent in Penwith, have also benefited populations of certain species such as coal tits and goldcrests, and provide nesting sites for buzzards, sparrowhawks and even, on occasion in the early stages of growth, the rare Montagu's harrier.

Black-headed gulls acquire the dark brown 'face' and white eye-ring of summer plumage before moving north to the breeding grounds.

Some of the old estates planted large gardens of exotic imports at a time when our own indigenous species were probably regarded as weeds or planted only for shelter. These gardens now hold many mature trees, and it is here that we find most of our woodland-dwelling wild things which have adapted to the imports. So, despite the supposed paucity of trees, we can find nearly all of the common British woodland species in such areas of Cornwall. In May a walk through Penrose, or Lanhydrock, for instance, will reveal some 20 species of bird, from woodpeckers to warblers. Fortunately, many so-called woodland species are much more creatures of the fringes, edges and clearings, rather than of otherwise continuous canopy. A walk up the Hayle river from St Erth in late April or early May might not be thought of as the ideal spot for woodland species yet I have recorded all the common residents in the one valley. Unfortunately, one of the exotic imports has become a menace to our woodland, the attractive but insidious *Rhododendron ponticum*. Where this spreads in a woodland, or even worse over a moor, the area becomes barren.

It is as well to emphasise again that little of the landscape of Cornwall is natural. Almost every square inch has been modified by man and his animals. Every prominent headland or carn has the remains of ancient settlements or forts still discernable among the gorse and bracken. Over the centuries the land has been broken-in, abandoned, broken again, mined and abandoned again by successive waves of agriculture and industry. Given time, nature will heal the ugly scars of man's endeavours and in these pockets of regeneration we can find some of the specialist plants, pioneers that manage to survive through the lack of competition in an alien environment. Some of the old mining areas are so contaminated with heavy metals and arsenic that few things are able to exist, yet those that do are among the most interesting and colourful, for the coarser perennials with deep tap-roots needing rich soil and moisture cannot survive here. Similarly, it is wind and salt that restrict the growth of broad-leaved competitors on the exposed coasts, resulting in the magnificent displays of thrift, kidney vetch and sea carrot.

St Ives Head, Pen Dynas or the Island, (which is an island only in the Cornish language sense, of an isolated place) might well be thought natural, but the huge rocks of the hill-fort tell of long occupation, as do the remains of boundary walls, old foundations and the more recent chapel and gun battery. Not so long ago, we boys used to throw rocks and fire airguns at the many rats, which swarmed over the rubbish dump. The car park has covered an area where the same boys used to pitch tents and sleep out for the summer and where before that there were chickens, pigs and goats. Were it not for the protests of a few enlightened people the town council at the time would have permitted parking over the whole headland. Bad enough, but they proposed worse than that! Nowadays, when in late spring the light from the setting sun illuminates the carpets of sea pinks on the western slopes, it is ablaze with colour. Later, there will be a glow of yellow from kidney vetch and bird's-foot trefoil and, at the end of summer, the hard white heads of sea carrot dotting the grassy slopes.

There are many other less conspicuous flowers here. In 1971, the Camborne/Redruth Natural History Society, under the guidance of Dr Stella Turk, made a detailed survey of all the wildlife on the Island and the resulting 32 pages of A4 are crammed with detailed information on everything from lichens to mammals. They found well over 100 species of flowering plants here and many grasses and lichens, apart from the seaweeds which are worthy of a study unto themselves. Presumably most are still here, despite the many feet which tread the ground in summer.

Late April, and these young ravens, attended by a parent with a throat pouch full of food, are ready to fly. With an incubation period of twenty-one days, and the young five or six weeks in the nest, they must have begun laying in mid-February.

Although there has been no recent survey, thirty years have seen many changes which might not be apparent to the present visitor to the Island. The pink thrift and sea carrot of the north slopes were here during the survey but were in isolated clumps and most of the ground was covered only in grass. The most interesting result of their study was not those plants which were recorded as present, but all those, so abundant elsewhere on the coast, which were entirely absent. I say that the only natural areas remaining in the county are the narrow strips between sea and field, the cliffs and salt-sprayed grasses of the low-lying coast. The vegetation of the Island, however, is not among those natural areas unmodified by man, far from it. Where else in the whole of Cornwall is such a coastal area totally free from heather, bluebells, gorse, and blackthorn? And where are the animals? There are no lizards, no slow-worms and no adders. Apart from the rats around the old dump, no other wild mammals seem to have been recorded for many years, and it is unlikely that any will come through the town. The survey found few slugs and not many snails, but that speciality of the Island, found nowhere else in Britain, the striped sandhill snail, was plentiful. Even thistles were uncommon and more or less confined to the ancient walls and rocky boundaries of early settlements on the south side. Rock pipits are the only breeding birds.

Jackdaws, deprived of breeding sites away from the cliffs as buildings are modernised or repaired, will readily take to nest boxes.

Those of us at the three-score-years-and-ten or more will remember even further back, to the 1930s when sea pinks were confined to the sea's edge, and there were hardly any other flowers to be found. The entire northern and western slope, and most of the south-eastern side of the Island was clothed only in grass, and mainly only one species at that. It was that narrow-leaved, thin wispy stuff that resists salt spray so well and survives where others perish, *Festuca rubra*, the red fescue. On the southern slopes opposite the gate, the only bloomers, apart from a few dandelions and daisies, were to be found among the washing spread out to dry in the sun on Mondays.

What caused this deficit among the flora, the lack of such common species as gorse and bracken, which are everywhere else? In those days, the parts of the Island that were not white with washing were black with drying nets. The nets were drying out from the thick pungent tanning of oak bark which preserved them from rotting in the long season when the fish, which they were designed to catch, were absent from the bay. They were taken from the vats of tanning and wheeled out there, still dripping, in long-handled barrows with wooden wheels, and spread over the ground to dry. I have no idea of how long this custom was observed, but it was for many years, possibly centuries. This

By late spring young herons, whose parents began the breeding cycle in winter, are already exploring streams and marshes.

tanning, 'bark' as we called it, rubbed from the nets as they were spread was, I believe, the first selective weedkiller regularly used by man in this area. Only the thin-leafed *Festuca rubra*, evolved to cope with intense saline conditions, could survive the regular light dosing of the poisonous, concentrated tanning and the sea spray. Everything else eventually succumbed.

The result was a unique, if restricted, community of flora, unparalleled anywhere else in the world. No doubt the insect community was also unique, with few caterpillars, for example, able to survive with such limited food plants, for hardly any butterflies were seen here. Maybugs, which we called dumble dories (they were not the proper dor beetle), were common but, as their larvae spend up to three years underground feeding on grass roots, of which there was an abundance, that was perhaps not surprising.

Now, as always with nature, things are changing. The effects of the tanning are decreasing, as it gradually leaches away. The south and eastern slopes produce an annual crop of coarse vegetation, which is regularly mowed (not to everyone's approval), and the sea pinks are magnificent. There is one bush of gorse, probably planted, as was the single pittosporum, brought over from the Isles of Scilly in the 1960s. Perhaps soon there will be a sprig of hawthorn from a passing redwing dropping a haw. A few sloes brought here might begin a colonisation of blackthorn. Heather might be welcome, but how would it arrive? And what about bracken, spread by spores? It will not be long before the changes accelerate, and a future survey might have to cope with thick bramble. Let us hope that heavy erosion from thousands of feet, together with the march of those dreaded established aliens the white onion flower and winter heliotrope, does not eliminate all the native species first.

At the end of spring, in May, our wild flowers are at their best, I think. Not that the flowers of summer are any less beautiful, just that in spring we have that exhilarating freshness about the countryside, with the bright greens emerging while the russet shades of winter linger. By now, the migrant birds have nearly all arrived and the chorus at dawn and dusk, and all night too at times, is at its height. Birdsong is ubiquitous now, if you are aware of it. Many years of leading parties of people on wildlife walks have demonstrated to me the remarkable capacity in the human ear for total deafness to wild sounds when there is nothing physically wrong with it. This, combined with the incredible inability of the human voice to remain silent, means that, for most people, birdsong is never heard. See a fox trotting along a track, a rabbit nibbling grass. The ears are never still; every rustle, every breath of wind and tweet of bird is heard and assessed before precipitating a reaction. Maybe there is too much noise in our world and, because we cannot listen to everything, we shut it all out, including the best music in the world, the songs of birds.

This is the time to hear, but not to learn, the individual songs. The miscellany of sound, in St Clement Woods or up the Treveal and Allen Valleys for instance, coming from maybe 20 species and all directions, is too confusing for beginners to separate specific songsters. In learning to identify birdsong it is best first to listen in winter, to the blackbirds in town or your garden. Listen, really listen, and then to the song thrush if you are lucky enough to have one near you still; the one fluty and languid, the other repetitive and rich. The plaintive robin next, then the vociferous wren and, as spring advances, hear the chaffinch in the woods, the skylark and whitethroat along the coastal paths, the reed warblers at Marazion. Learn them one at a time and they will bring you joy for the remainder of your days.

Gorse clump. Yellow gorse can dazzle the eye and fill the nose with heady perfume on warm sunny days.

The noises from the spring migrants are not all songs. Some, as with those of autumn, are just call-notes from a bush or high in the sky. Some experience and skill is required to recognise these sounds but, to hear and know the haunting call of the whimbrel, say, that whistling tremolo overhead or from a flock resting in a favoured field, such as the slopes of Gwithian Towans when they arrive in the last week of April, is enthralling. Like the first cuckoo, or a grasshopper warbler reeling at Zennor, all the migrants tell us, with their individual voices, that they are safely home again. In late May the swifts are here and it is time too to hear that last and most ethereal of the summer bird sounds to delight us. Choose a warm and balmy evening, windless, in late May and June, and walk across the downs to the slopes of some heather-covered hill. Or you can be lazy and try Carn Galver. Park by the Bosigran engine houses. Stop and listen as the dusk falls about you. There! Or is it there? Somewhere up there? Or on the next bit of our fragmented moorland? Ah, there! Chuurrrrr-urrrr-urrrr-urrrr-urrr. Nightjars… Magic!

Hell's Mouth. Seabirds return to their nesting ledges in late winter and spend more time there as the days lengthen. Seals breed in the caves under the cliffs.

These cormorants nesting along the ridge at Hell's Mouth are unperturbed by gales or crashing waves. At the end of April most had tiny young or chipping eggs after some thirty days of incubation. Even at this stage the whole site is plastered in guano and, by the time the young leave, the smell is unbearable. Does it serve some purpose, such as powerful insecticide? Just a thought…

A typical deep zawn, or inlet, in the cliffs. The ledges in these sheltered clefts are used for nesting by shags and crows alike.

By late May some areas of cliff are a mass of colour.

This prominent flat-topped rock is a typical buzzards' 'larder' where prey is brought for dismembering and preparation before being taken to the nest. It is always worth scanning such prominences for signs of use – bits of rabbit fur or a dead vole.

These remains, on an anthill used as a latrine by foxes, were left by a buzzard.

Closer inspection reveals the leg and skin of a toad.

Sea pinks, which I think a far more evocative name than 'thrift', contrast their exquisite colour with the blue of the ocean. Here they thrive in thick, dark humus brought to the surface by ants.

A sheltered clump is likely to be swamped by more vigorous plants eventually.

Not all clumps of distant 'sea campion' are as they seem. Here is the 'kill-site' of a peregrine falcon. Like buzzards, peregrines have their favourite places for plucking and preparing prey.

Inset: *Sea campion. A truly characteristic plant of our cliffs in spring and one of the earliest, it usually grows in thick clumps, visible from far away.*

In sheltered valleys the hawthorn grows in perfect symmetry, and in late May and early June swathes the slopes in white blossom.

Swans are now in full splendour, with fresh white plumage. The cobs can be particularly aggressive at this time of year but old yarns about their wings having the power to break a man's arm should be taken with a large dose of salt.

Cott Valley, St Just, is one of the 'western valleys' where bird-watchers expect to find the early migrants. Here it is infested with Japanese knotweed, white three-cornered leek and montbretia, the terrible three, which, together with the purple rhododendron, are a serious threat to the Cornish wild flora.

Bluebells still survive on the sunny side of the track while three-cornered leek has wiped them out on the shady side. Since these photographs were taken, the National Trust and the Cornwall Environmental Trust have done a superb job of clearing the knotweed from the valley with funding from landfill tax. Money well spent.

In spring, male starlings are in full iridescent colour and show the blue base to their bills.

Far left: *Black plumage and yellow bill denote a male blackbird. It is one of our finest songsters with its rich fluty cadences.*

Left: *Female blackbirds build their grass-lined nests in thick garden shrubs, but not always well enough hidden to escape the predatory magpie.*

One of two stone carvers and poets was probably responsible for this charming signpost at Treen on the B3306: either the Zennor poet and stone carver Henry Quick or his rival poet and carver Billy Foss of Sancreed. While resting here you might look out for birds of prey: buzzards, kestrels, harriers and short-eared owls.

Tater-du lighthouse surrounded by the little quillets (small fields) of the early flower and potato growers of a hundred years ago. It was here that I found a magnificent gyr falcon on my seventieth birthday.

While out to check cormorants at Hell's Mouth, I learned of this wreck, smashed in two by the previous night's gale, with the sea now unbelievably calm a few hours after such ferocity. Despite the wind, the cormorants' nests on the nearby ridge were completely undamaged.

Grotesque granite megaliths, carved by wind, time and temperature, with bluebells at their base, perch precariously over the south coast near St Loy.

Carn Galver, in 2000, after a late winter fire. All was apparently devastated but the ground was still moist and the burnout on the surface only. Inset left: Bluebells emerge from the ashes, their bulbs safe deep beneath the mould. Inset right: Rosebay willowherb, or fireweed, lives up to its name and is one of the first colonisers after a fire. It is when the ground is dry down to bedrock that severe damage, taking years to repair, is done to the moorland.

From the ancient ramparts of the hill-fort of Caer Bran (Raven's Castle) we can see right across to the Lizard in the east. A good spot, on fine spring days, from which to watch displaying buzzards over their territories all about you.

Botallack labyrinth, where the first crude smelting drew arsenic from the ore, and men crawled through the tunnels as they cooled, scraping it from the walls. The area is now regenerating with plants that can survive the pollution that remains and will eventually neutralise its effects. Nature is always the greatest healer, given time.

While considered remote, I have counted over a hundred people walking over this bridge at Porthmeor in a couple of hours. The stream is a good spot for damselflies and the many butterflies that will draw nectar from the stands of hemp-agrimony later in the year.

*Early spring can bring many surprises but this scene at a Cornish estuary on the first
of April was a sure sign of what happens when we fool about with the climate.*

By late spring the cove-boats of Penberth are ready for the mackerel shoals, also followed by gannets and dolphins. The narrow valleys leading inland from the coves offer shelter to tired migrants in spring and autumn.

Summer is a time for beaches and there is always plenty of wildlife to hold our attention. On fine days such as this, it is easy to spot basking sharks and dolphins as they patrol the coasts, while migrating terns call to each other as they pass.

HAF

SUMMER

Come out, come out, this summer day,
The fields are sweet with new-mown hay,
The birds are singing loud and clear,
For summer-time once more is here;

Hay-time C.M. Lowe

The summer months are those of barbecues, beaches, and buckets and spades. We may not see much wildlife at a barbecue, other than a few midges in the smoke, but the beaches are full of interesting creatures, either along the strand-line or in the rock pools left by the receding tide. No family visit to the seashore is complete without a net and a jamjar with which to catch and view them. Later, the urge to hunt and catch develops into the less intrusive pleasure of simply observing, when just lying beside a pool and looking into its depths is to be transported into another world.

Spearmint, a flower of pond edges and marshy ground is a great attraction for several species of butterfly.

Rock pools are fascinating. During spring tides, when they are fully exposed, we have just an hour or two to explore them and each one is unique. A variation in depth or shade or angle to the sun will result in a completely different spectrum of life and two pools, side by side, are like different worlds to peer into but, as a general rule, the lower the pool, the more diverse the life. They vary from little cups of water that are filled by spray and dry out on each tide, leaving an encrustation of salt glittering in the sun, to pools deep enough to dive into. To spend time gazing into these is to be mesmerised by colour and form, by tranquillity and silence in the depths. I learned to swim in such a pool, where only the highest tides refreshed the water, which warmed up daily in summer. It was not a good pool for marine life. Like others which are too high above the sea, it became too warm and a thin trickle of fresh water seeping from the cliff diluted the salinity. Only a thin covering of green *enteromorpha* seaweed grew around the edges, which in turn supported a few limpets living at the upper limit of their distribution.

Pools at all levels, from those at the splash zone right down to those exposed only at the lowest springs, reveal an amazing diversity of life. At the top, among the small cups of salt-saturated, rapidly evaporating water and what appears to be a band of barren rock, dwell thousands of creatures that emerge mainly at night. These are the sea-slaters, those maritime relatives of woodlice, that we knew only by the name of gramma sows, maybe a corruption of the Kernewek gwraghas. They scavenge among the detritus thrown up by the waves and, together with other rock-dwelling marine crustaceans, the slender springtails, are at the bottom end of a food chain that sustains rock pipits, turnstones, purple sandpipers and even lizards which are sometimes found among the sparse vegetation of the splash zone. Whimbrel may also be seen thrusting their long bills deep into rock crevices when they pause on their migration north. Pools that are just too high to be swilled out by the action of waves, especially if a trickle of fresh water runs into them, are full of such crustaceans, and a little bit of food dropped in (they seem to like orange peel) will draw them out into the open.

Pools that are replenished with seawater on the top of every tide do not, at first sight, appear to have much life in them. Here, however, is yet another indication of nature's ability to colonise every possible habitat with vibrant life. Even the walls of these little pools show no bare rock and are covered in algae. To quote from *A Handbook of the Natural History of The Lizard Peninsula*, 'All the rock pools are lined with encrusting stony seaweeds (*Lithothamniae*) as evenly and completely as an earthenware container may be glazed to the rim.' Perfect!

Usually there is little green seaweed, for the browsing limpets eat it all except for the tuft that each one carries on its own shell, safe from those rasping mouths. It is difficult to comprehend the amount of green seaweed limpets devour. In 1967 after the wreck of the *Torrey Canyon,* when all the limpets, together with everything else, were killed off by detergents, the first recolonisers of the utterly barren shore were the green seaweeds. With no limpets to eat it, the weed coloured the whole rocky coast from Newquay to Falmouth in a lurid green until the shellfish gradually recolonised and reduced it to normal levels.

Further down, either in pools that do not dry out, or on wet gullies in the shade, the pink encrustations of the calcareous pink algae, *Lithothamniae*, colour both pool and rock. The colours of these rock pools are truly spectacular and the creatures that live in them are, in their strange and miniature way, among the most peculiar yet most beautiful in nature. Some are so bizarre as to be from the realms of science fiction and a search among the weed and boulders at the very edge of low springs will reveal creatures so strange as to seem from another world, as indeed they are. Not all is colour though! I was once shown, in a pool at Rinsey, hundreds of tiny jellyfish, about a centimetre in diameter, which were totally transparent and almost invisible until pointed out.

We are fortunate in having access to many such pools on all types of shore. From the serpentine rock of Kynance, by way of the flat slate-beds of Prussia Cove, the causeway to St Michael's Mount, low tide at Cape Cornwall, to the granite of Treveal Cove opposite the Western Carracks, right past Godrevy Head, each site is unique. Wave action and sunshine are very different at Porthcrew, by Rinsey Head, from those at the shady bottom of the cliffs on the north coast. The most beautiful pools that are just uncovered at every tide, which is just above the level of low-water neap tides. There is so much to see and marvel at. There are some 25 species of crab to identify, and some 200 fish recorded in Cornwall, though few of the latter will be found in rock pools. Here are the blennies and gobies, just quick blurs as they dash away for cover at the least shadow falling on their pool. By staying still, we may try to identify them by the shape of the dorsal fins when they emerge again and lie in the sunshine's glitter on the submerged rock faces.

The strand-line is the place to search for seashells. Here again, each beach is almost unique in its accumulation of creatures and flotsam. Marazion seems to attract the most weed and litter, being exposed to the southerlies, and there are sometimes treasures to be found amongst the junk, such as mermaids' purses (the egg cases of skate, rays dogfish etc.), Chinaman's hats (the small conical shell *Calytraea chinensis*), West Indian beans (large seeds of tropical American trees) that may have taken two years to drift across the Atlantic, and cuttlebones for your canary (and your tadpoles, by the way). Only on the more exposed beaches at Porthcurnow have I found the tiny blue-rayed limpet with its three stripes of fluorescent turquoise. Here, also, by searching along the strand-line, may be found the delightful little spotted cowrie shells, perfect miniatures of the huge ones found in tropical seas. The beach is almost entirely comprised of broken shell, the most common being trough shells, a

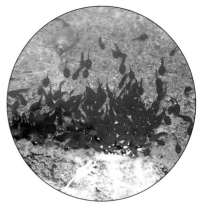

Tadpoles of the common toad. In garden ponds toads thrive better than frogs, for whom the surrounding areas are often much too dry, but in our acidic water are sometimes slow to develop. These guys are swarming on to powdered cuttlebone, evidently hungry for the rich sea salts and calcium to supplement their diet.

kind of cockle that lives in coarse sands and clean water. It was here that I found the only live necklace shell I have seen; they must be, common offshore, however, for many trough shells are washed up bearing the neat, tell-tale hole through which they were eaten by the predatory necklaces that live by boring holes in other shellfish. Porthkidney and Gwithian have the widest variety of shells on them, from common mussels to scallops, top shells and the lovely pink tellins.

During winter storms whole beaches can disappear on one tide, with thousands of tons of sand and all the shells and marine invertebrates dragged out to below low-water level. Onshore winds take the sand out, offshore winds bring it back, the latter taking much longer than the former. Groundswells crash, churn up the sand and surge onwards, dropping the grains at the top of the beach as the impetus is expended and the surge slowly recedes. Wind-driven waves are lower, break further up the beach in churning curls and drag the sand down. It is true that groundswells will sometimes bite into accumulated sand, leaving a small cliff where beachcombers look for lost pennies and gold rings, but the overall action of such weather in the long run is to bring sand in. It is quite interesting to watch the opposite results of different waves, however small they may be, in differing weather conditions. All these spots are well worth a visit, but please remember to leave things as you find them, with stones replaced and animals returned to whence they came. In addition, check the tide tables and keep your eye on the waves. There is no such thing as a freak one, they are all dangerous.

While walking the cliff paths at any time of year we should also keep a lookout for our largest mammal, the Atlantic, or grey, seal. A metre long at birth, the bulls are massive creatures when seen up close and I am never quite sure if those sharp teeth are entirely harmless when approached by one while swimming in an isolated cove. As with herring gulls, seals were regularly shot before and especially during the war and consequently became very wary. When I used to see them on the Western Carracks, off Treveal, while fishing for pollack in the late 1940s, they would lumber off the rocks at the approach of the boat and all disappear below the surface, not to be seen again, as they can stay submerged for twenty minutes. Then, when we were taking tourists on trips around the bay and fishing parties after mackerel, one enterprising boatman always seemed to book more passengers than anyone else. His secret was soon out, however. He had discovered a new geographical feature that everyone else had completely overlooked for centuries: Seal Island, a new name for the

Caterpillar of broom moth on gorse.

Low water, spring tide. Now is the time to look for sea creatures, such as crabs and 'whistle fish', the bearded rockling, that can only be found among the kelp and oar weed. The rock in the distance is called Carrack an Ydhyn, Rock of the Birds.

Western Carracks! He had started what was probably the first eco-tourist venture in Cornwall, and it is still running. By approaching slowly, the St Ives boatmen gained the confidence of the seals, which soon learned to lie in the sun with complete indifference as our boats came within a few feet of the rocks and cameras clicked off miles of film. In those days I saw up to 30 seals sprawled out, depending on the wind and tide, but the numbers appear to have diminished there recently. Nevertheless, seals are still common all around the peninsula and may be observed from dry land at favourite spots: Boscastle, the North Cliffs, Godrevy, the Western Carracks, Porthgwarra and the Lizard. There were 117 recently counted lying out at an inaccessible cove. They usually breed during late summer and autumn in sea caves but, with increasing tameness, have given birth to pups, as in former times, on shingle beaches beneath the cliffs where they may be observed from the paths.

Passenger boats ply to the Western Carracks, 'Seal Island'.

There is no doubt that in summer or winter the seashore presents us with enough interesting wildlife to keep us totally absorbed, but other delights await elsewhere.

Summer in the country means swallows. In town, it is swifts. Everyone welcomes the sight of their first swallow. The first arrivals come in March and often go to water, where they spend long hours flying to and fro as they dip to catch the myriad gnats emerging from the winter's mud. Farmers look for them around barns, where the diet is more of flies, but they will take any insect small enough to eat. They begin nesting very soon after arriving, and when they settle in they are there for the season, seldom venturing more than 200 metres from the nest when feeding young.

We are reaching the stage when increasing numbers of species depend on the direct intervention of man for their survival. Although our track-record of destruction of things natural is a sad indictment of our short-sightedness, man's activities have also indirectly benefited a number of species all over the world by providing food and breeding sites where none existed naturally. Nearly all the purple martins in eastern North America breed in nest boxes provided by people. Some of the boxes resemble blocks of flats with a hundred or more holes and compartments. This has been happening for many years, beginning with the indigenous people who hung up large gourds to provide a base in which the birds could build. In Cornwall our small population of pied flycatchers and other woodland species depend on nest boxes in over-managed woods where old timber is cleared away and not allowed to develop natural cavities. Swallows and house martins, too, have become almost entirely dependent on buildings for nesting. And then there are owls in barns, jackdaws in chimneys, gulls on roofs, sparrows in the eaves, and, of course, bats in the belfry.

For these species a good home for the future seemed assured as long as man was around to provide the nooks and crannies. Alas, they had not reckoned with building regulations, European directives, improvement grants or even central heating. Most of the barns have been converted, chimneys are becoming obsolete, eaves are draught-proofed, belfries blocked, old mine buildings pointed up, and shafts covered over, all with a loss of sites and a decline in populations. Unless they can adapt, swallows are about to suffer a drastic decline, for regulations decreed by 'EU-know-who' will mean that they are no longer allowed to nest where cattle are milked, or food stored, for fear of spreading disease; unbelievable, when milk is sealed from teat to tank to pasteurisation with no chance of contamination. Where will they go? Their numbers are certain to decline and the flies, of which they consume millions, to increase proportionately, perhaps. Possibly as a consequence of being excluded from their ancestral barn, a pair of swallows bred in the public toilet on the coast road at Morvah in 2001. Another pair began nesting in the underground fogou at Carn

Euny in 2000. Maybe it was the first time they had bred there since a directive of the Roman 'EU', Number XDVIII – *Pro bono publico. Exeunt avis* [get out, birds!] banned them from nesting in fogous for hygienic reasons in about AD301.

It may be hard to imagine a spring with no swallows, but who would have thought that a common old sparrow would ever become a rare sight in the countryside? However, by providing a nesting site, usually in the form of a box, which does not have to be expensive, we can do much to slow the decline of most hole nesters, and nest boxes are used by thousands of birds every year. Autumn and winter is the time to put them up. Even a small box on a town house will accommodate sparrows, a bigger one starlings. Yes, starlings are declining too. In larger gardens or in the countryside, tits, robins, flycatchers and even thrushes will move in. A large box will be welcomed by kestrels, barn owls and tawny owls. Almost any type will be used, for, given half a chance, species will maintain themselves if the habitat is suitable. After my neighbour had removed two chimneys from her property and I modernised my cottage with the consequent loss of another, the local jackdaws were out of house and home. To compensate them, I put up some nest boxes, which were occupied within twenty-four hours. As a result the grateful jackdaws came down to my vegetable garden and ate up all my peas. There's no justice, is there? Swifts are essentially townies. Nearly all the thousands of European swifts nest in houses, having benefited enormously from the development of towns and cities, one of the very few species to have done so. They like large old terraced houses with gable-ends or ill-fitting fascia boards where they can have a clear run-in and a short scramble to a suitable crevice or a hollow under the eaves. Most of them seem to be Methodists, for they prefer chapels rather than churches. Despite their original nest sites being in crevices in trees and cliffs, I know of no swifts breeding out in our countryside now, although a few formerly bred in crevices on the North Cliffs. They arrive late and depart early, needing the high density of high-flying insects found only in summer at our latitude, and they also spend much time swooping over water on arrival and before departing in August, especially when strong winds inhibit high-flying insects. Unlike swallows, however, they are great travellers, even after arrival, flying many miles from the nest in search of food as they circumnavigate depressions to stay in fine weather. They spend their whole lives airborne, eating, sleeping and even mating on the wing, needing terra firma only for a nesting site.

When I first began noting the habits of birds in Cornwall, particularly in west Cornwall, nesting house martins were quite a rarity, breeding in my parish only

Aeshna juncea, the common hawker, is widely distributed in western Britain. Very fast on the wing, dragonflies are easiest to identify and photograph if found copulating, which is something of a protracted business in Aeshna species. The common hawker flies in late summer, July to September, and prefers open moorland and heaths.

under the eaves of the large farmhouses built by Sir Edward Hain in the first decade of the twentieth century. These were the only houses in suitable positions with overhanging roofs and a soffit, for the traditional Cornish house had only a fascia board beneath the ovice (bottom rows of slate) which suited swifts but not martins. House martins still breed on these farmhouses, as long as they are not smothered in ivy or Virginia creeper, but they have also taken advantage of the new style of building with an overhang and have spread into the expanding bungalow developments around most towns. Their nests are protected by law, although I suppose if they were to be knocked down in the night by an irate householder, upset by the mess they make, more than a few neighbours would be in sympathy. When feeding with swallows, martins tend to fly higher and take more aphids but, here in Cornwall, many take advantage of onshore breezes and feed along the low cliffs and over the coves.

A few sand martins breed in the earth cliffs at Perranuthnoe and along the similar cliffs at Gwithian. They are the first of the swallow tribe to arrive, being seen over water, as at Marazion and Stithians, where they feed by fluttering into the wind low over the surface. Many a sand martin is reported as an early swallow by those who have not yet learned the difference.

Wildlife is not all about the birds and bees and bugs and butterflies. There is something for everyone in Cornwall, from whales to whirligigs, most of which can be completely overlooked. And size isn't everything either. It is much easier to see a tiny whirligig spinning about on the surface tension of some stagnant pond than to see the giant whales that pass by, and sometimes stay offshore for a few days, every year. At the time of writing, I have never seen one of the biggies, but I did see a killer whale off the north coast some years ago.

The amount of life in seawater is staggering. One cubic metre of the stuff contains literally millions of plankton, tiny diatoms and dinoflagellates of 0.01 mm in diameter, too small for us to see so the water appears clear and sterile. Yet everything in the sea right up to the great whales depends upon it. The plankton under a given area of seawater weighs more than the crops grown on the same area of land. This seems hard to believe on those rare days in summer when the sun shines down from blue skies and the view to the horizon from some headland reveals nothing but the glassy surface for as far as the eye can see. On such windless days the white clouds are reflected with such brilliance as to pain the eye, and the only movement is at the meeting of the tides, where dark swirls and ripples mark the ebb and flow unruffled by opposing breezes. The whole of the ocean seen from cliff or beach appears devoid of life from the shore to the far horizon. Where are all the living things that a change in the wind will bring close to shore in their hundreds? There are no passing shearwaters, no splashes from plunging gannets, and even the gulls sit lethargically on the rocks and roofs. It is as if the ocean has been deserted. But that is nothing but deception. Soon there will be movement. Objects begin to appear in the distance. Ships glide by on the horizon, the low-frequency throb of their engines reaching quiet shores as more of a vibration than sound. Yachtsmen caught in the doldrums start their outboards and whistle for wind. Vague movements in the distance resolve into the flags of crab pots, hanging limp on poles angled by the tide. Shags raise their wings and sit back on the water before taking off in an effort of pattering feet with no uplift from a passing breeze.

Now is the time to look carefully at that apparently empty ocean. There is no better time than on these still days to find those creatures that live under the water and reveal themselves to us only as brief glimpses of dorsal fin or tail as they break the surface for air: dolphins, porpoises and whales, which are almost impossible to see when the surface is disturbed by wind and wave. After their apparent absence for many years, I saw a pod of unidentified dolphins off Pendeen on 25 May 1987. There were about ten individuals, swimming evenly in tight formation, with a single young one in front occasionally leaping clear of the surface. After moving east for about half a mile they turned and swam west, when some of the larger ones also leapt clear of the surface from time to time as they increased speed. Typical bottle–nosed behaviour as we learned later. They were not recorded again until 1991 when a pod of over 30 turned up and have been recorded annually ever since, although the pod has split up or their numbers diminished to less than ten here now. Most of my own records are from October to March but they can be seen at any time of year, sometimes putting on an extra performance for the audience at the Minack Theatre.

Porpoises are also more likely to be seen when the sea is glassy-smooth, for their brief roll, which reveals only a low dorsal fin on a small cetacean half the size of a dolphin, breaks the surface for mere seconds. They are very difficult to find when there is even the slightest disturbance on the surface. Once very common here, they are now rare but apparently increasing; one or two can be seen when conditions are right. But whales? Oh yes! They are seen regularly off the Cornish coast. Pilot whales are occasionally washed ashore and were in

Sea plantain. This relative of the common weed of your lawn is an elegant little plant when growing in the harsh conditions of a spray-washed cliff.

attendance on the mackerel shoals during the times of abundance in the 1970s. Orcas, the killer whales, are also seen from time to time, and the big ones, the minke and fin whales are now regularly recorded around Land's End by patient watchers in winter. A high vantage point and good optics are needed to see these big fellows, for they stay far out.

But that other monster with the massive dorsal followed by an equally massive tail, which swirls so far behind it as to be thought another creature, can be seen with the naked eye on calm summer days. These basking sharks, which come and go from no-one-knows-where to pass by in the summer, are the most easily found of the sea creatures which might be seen from shore. On calm days the gliding fins and huge white mouths break the surface with an extraordinary elegance for such enormous creatures, and can be seen from afar. From time to time they breach, leaping high into the air and falling back into the sea with an enormous splash and a reverberating smack that can be heard a mile away. They seem to be increasingly common and it is not now exceptional to see half a dozen from a single headland. Look for them along the converging currents where the plankton is brought to the surface. Another large fin, flopping about as though it were a useless appendage or on a dead thing, is the high, narrow dorsal of *Mola mola,* the sunfish, which can grow as large as 3.3m (11 feet) long in tropical waters. Those that reach us are usually less than a metre in length and come very close inshore, being frequently seen below the Island lookout at St Ives and off most of the headlands in late summer and autumn, apparently at the mercy of the tides. At times they appear almost dead, but are merely floating passively and are very often attended by a sitting herring gull, picking them clean of parasites.

All these creatures – and sometimes, even a turtle if you are very lucky – are to be seen on what appears at first to be an empty ocean. And then a gannet appears! High in the sky on a windless day it banks sharply and turns into a dive, shoots down and slices into the glossy sheen and disappears amidst a shower of spray and droplets glittering in the sunshine. Nothing to see? Too calm? That'll be the day!

The gannet has to be one of our most spectacular birds. Were they rare they would draw huge crowds to see them, and I am thankful that it is impossible to keep them in zoos. In 1995 I was runner-up in the BBC *Wildlife Magazine* Awards for Nature Writing with an article on gannets. I can do no better to introduce you to this wonderful bird than by quoting the article here...

SETHORYON

Gannets once bred on islands off Cornwall but, in those harsher times, were over-exploited for their eggs and young and exterminated by my ancestors. They are still familiar birds to us Cornish, nevertheless, and their passage along the coast has been long recorded. This is almost continuous; varying from a few birds, barely visible over the horizon during spells of fine weather, to over a thousand an hour during westerly gales in autumn, when they are often so close we can see their pale eyes from the shore. Most of these birds fly steadfastly on, the young migrating south and the adults to the wintering areas nearer the breeding colonies. Some will be merely relocating after displacement by severe weather during the hours of darkness and will fish leisurely in the bays as they return to their offshore stations.

Only very severe and protracted storms will tire them to the extent that they are driven downwind in daylight. The fiercer the gale, the lower they fly, gliding along the still air in the troughs and above force seven on the Beaufort Scale, when the white spume flies from the tips of the waves; they hug the swells like shearwaters, careening over the peaks with the momentum gathered from the uplift of air on the passing rollers, even plunging at times through the foam of the breaking crests and continuing in their flight unchecked.

During winter, the young are off the west coast of Africa and the older birds in the North Atlantic. It seems that during this period they spread themselves thinly across wide areas of ocean. I have watched them soaring high over calm seas, circling alone or as individuals in small, widely-spaced parties, slowly quartering the surface with occasional checks and tight circles in their flight as they search the dark waters. On some days in the Western Approaches they might be thought rare in the area, so few are encountered.

Like many terrestrial species, seabirds have adapted their normal behaviour to exploit the activities of man, and gannets will wait in attendance upon the fishing fleet, as gulls follow the plough. The trawlers may drag their nets for an hour, two hours, steaming slowly ahead, while crews rest and birds pass them by indifferently. Before there are any men on deck, or there is any indication from the boats that the winches are due to haul the nets, I have watched the birds gather, waiting on the surface or hanging in the air above the stern. They know, by some learned, observed or innate perception, when the trawls are about to surface, and they swoop down on them in a

In some years tortoiseshell butterflies are quite scarce until late summer and autumn, when the broods descended from early immigrants, or the few that hibernated through the winter, emerge to feed on garden flowers. This was one of 25 at a time found on one small Pileostegia viburnoides, *one of the best garden climbers for attracting insects, especially hoverflies, butterflies and bees.*

grunting rabble, snatching the small fish from the sea or the nets as they slip through the meshes.

However, although apparently undescribed in the literature, it is when the gannets feed on shoals in open waters that the true magnificence of their fishing methods can be appreciated and, during the winter months, especially in January and February when the south-westerlies drive the frosts from Cornwall and the sprat into the bays, the gannets always follow, and it is a joy to observe them fishing close to shore. Those solitary birds, soaring high over the ocean like vultures over a desert, watch their neighbours; way off in the distance a dive incites that curiosity and a close approach which is seen by the next neighbour, and the next. Soon, there are dozens, hundreds, at times thousands, of white, black-tipped wings, for they are all adults here now, and the feasting begins.

The birds feed into the wind and form an orderly queue, sometimes over a mile or more in length, which advances as it rises, with the birds gradually gaining height until they are above the shoal. When the fish are deep below the surface the dives are high, with the slowly advancing ranks utilising the wind to reach the peak of the climbing procession, so that the movement of birds is like a rolling white conveyor-belt, with the birds rising slowly to the apex. From here they dive. They will hang in the air, waiting for the opportune moment when the fish are visible, and then turn into the plunge, guiding themselves to the target with half-open wings, falling like a shower of missiles on to the fish. Then, after bouncing to the surface, they peel off in twin streams, like bombers from a squadron, and fly downwind to rejoin the endless succession of birds ascending. At times the falling birds are so close together, with plumes of spray rising high behind them as they slice into the surface, that injury from those dagger bills seems inevitable. Gannet after gannet will plummet into the mass of fish, calling excitedly to each other with their harsh voices rising above the noise of the wind as they plunge through flights of kittiwakes, auks and gulls, yet they never strike another.

At times, the sprat are driven by larger fish, which are preyed upon in turn by dolphins circling the shoals and leaping from the water below the wheeling birds. When driven so, the fishes break the surface in a threshing mass of spray and the gannets will dive again and again, often rising no more than a foot or two from the surface; a couple of wing beats and once more down into the silver feast until eventually replete, too full to fly, they sit in parties on the sea, paddling into the wind.

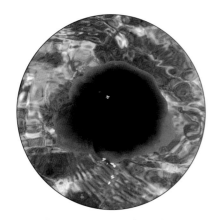

Jellyfish have an ethereal beauty not often appreciated when their tentacles leave a nasty wheal on the skin. Two species are often washed up on beaches in summer, this one, that I think is Cyanea lamarckii, *and the common blue or so-called moon jellyfish,* Aurelia aurita, *similar but with four dark rings. The latter is one of several species that sometimes come inshore in vast numbers. The stings of the blue ones are not particularly severe, but detached filaments of the larger brown species* Cyanea capillata *cause acute rashes on the arms of fishermen hauling nets. In northern seas this species can reach two metres in diameter.*

The Cornish for this magnificent bird is 'An Sethor', The Archer, plural 'Sethoryon', for these diving flocks are reminiscent of a shower of arrows shot from a thousand bows. And now, while the colonies to the north become increasingly overcrowded, and migrants pass so close to our inaccessible stacks, I watch them approach those abandoned ledges and hope that some day the descendants of those earlier Cornish Bowmen will forgive us our trespasses against them, recolonise their ancestral sites, and breed here unmolested.

———•◆•———

Cornwall is as a fortress, surrounded by walls of solid stone. From the towering cliffs at Beeny, with breaks at the bays, the slates and blue elvans become granite, with a few greenstone outcrops protruding as dark headlands, such as Carrick Du and Tater-du, right around to Newlyn. From Marazion the serpentine of the Lizard peninsula leads on to the granite and slates of the south coast to complete the fortification. So, maybe in the heat of summer, if we get any, comes the time for less active pursuit of wildlife, and even for those who don't want, or are unable, to follow the more strenuous paths there is still plenty to see. Lie down and study the rocks.

Green, grey, red, black, the rocks are of many hues, but it is not always obvious just what the basic colour of the cliffs and carns might be. That which appears to be a landscape tinted by geology is often not the case. Bare surfaces are difficult to find in nature. From below sea level to the highest carns there are forms of life, which colonise and coat the rocks. The barnacles are the most obvious, smothering all in their buff shells to high-water level. Above these, on a steep cliff, say, there is a narrow area of bare rock where the abrasive action of wave and sand grind the surface clean. From this level upwards the whole rock face is colonised by some of the most lowly yet most interesting forms of life, the lichens.

There is a nature reserve where a prominent sign informs visitors of the average time taken to complete the circuit of boardwalks. Average time for walkers – half an hour. Families with children – one hour. Bird-watchers, allow three hours! It is an area of wetland where the birds are mainly waders and other LBJs (little brown jobs) that take some time to identify by examining fine details of plumage, colour of bills and legs, and call notes. They are bird-watchers' birds, for only the cognoscenti appreciate the significance of what they are seeing. The sign is, in fact, too optimistic. It would take a full day to see and identify all the birds in such an area. Bird-watchers do not therefore make good companions for walkers who want to stride out, heads down, and get from Perranporth to Gwithian in a day. Botanists are even slower, especially when confronted by the complex terrestrial orchids that emerge from the Cornish earth in summer. Be thankful, however, that your walking-partner is unlikely to be a lichenologist. Those who are captivated by this little-known subject have been known to lie on a rock for hours at a time, like those left for dead or mistaken for discarded statues, with their little magnifying glass up to a squinted eye.

Comprising a symbiosis between fungi and algae, the lichens are a fascinating group to study. They, like all forms of life, do not grow and survive at random. Our towering cliffs, such as those that rise from sea level at Porthcurnow, are colonised by a succession of species, if that is what they are, which specialise in occupying succeeding levels. After the bare rock above the barnacles comes the wide band of black encrustations of *Verrucarias*. Above this those familiar orange-yellow circles of *Caloplacas* which grow out like fairy rings of mushrooms. Then comes the band of grey-green filaments which thrive in the most exposed situations to exploit the minute nutrients brought on rain and wind, the *Ramalinas*. Among the *Ramalinas* may occasionally be found the similar, but much rarer, *Roccellas*, but these will only be distinguished by the expert. Topping all on peaks and isolated rocks is the bright yellow crown of *Xanthorias* which exploit the rich nutrients in the droppings of birds.

This is a very simplified example of distribution. Local factors such as sun or shade, and exposure, will determine where individual species grow, and there is ruthless competition among them, as in all of nature. The one essential for a rich lichen flora is clean air. The slightest pollution will inhibit their survival, and an examination of surfaces on which they grow, from church towers to tree trunks, will indicate very accurately the degree of pollution in a given area. In Cornwall we still have relatively pure air, which is one of the reasons why lichens are so prolific here.

The exquisite beauty of the lichens can really only be appreciated to the full by lying prone and studying them with the aid of a small magnifying glass or hand lens. Few of them have English names, but don't be put off by impossible-seeming scientific ones. They are easy to learn from the excellent field guides now available in every subject of natural history but, if you do become interested in, and eventually absorbed by, the study of lichen, please carry a little card or plaque telling passers-by not to be alarmed, that you are alive and well and studying *Buellia subdisciformis*. They will be much relieved.

Sunbathing is an activity that many species enjoy. Foxes revel in the warm rays and will sleep in the sun if they think they are unobserved. I saw one walk a few paces, have a quick lie down, then walk a few more paces before having another quick dose of sun on its belly before moving on, evidently torn between a doze in the sensuous sunshine and the risk of being caught unawares. Buzzards, as well as many small birds, will lie flat on their bellies, with feathers raised to get the sun on their skins, and I saw a peregrine lying on its back doing the same when to my astonishment its mate flew in beside it and they both stretched out in the sun. They do not normally be so close together except occasionally at the nest or when actually mating, for the female is a bit of a bully and her mate somewhat wary of approaching her uninvited. When the sun shines, collared doves will perform similar antics to get the sunshine on their underwings, raising one wing after the other to get the warm rays on the normally concealed feathers.

This shot of a young robin sunbathing was taken by a friend, John Johns, and is one of those wonderful opportunistic shots, showing some aspect of bird behaviour, that we dream of taking. Many species enjoy a sunbathe.

The first collared dove was recorded in Cornwall in 1959. Since then they have become widespread and are common in most towns. Indeed, they are a commensal of man, dependent on parks and gardens in urban areas. In the wild countryside they are quite uncommon and even then are seen mainly about farms and grain stores where I have seen over 50 settled on a barn roof, hanging about in the hope of spillage. This was in October, so some of them may have been migrants. Living in towns, on bread and crumbs of saffron cake, they would presumably suffer from vitamin deficiencies and be as unfit as some of the pathetic pigeons searching for sustenance among the feet of pedestrians. That which appears to be easy picking is not always of benefit to any of us. From time to time I have seen collared doves on the seashore and wondered what they were doing there below the high-tide line, but then I saw one individual eating the green seaweed (*Enteromorpha*) which coats the exposed rocks. It spent some three minutes selecting and swallowing long strands. Since then I have observed that this is quite a regular occurrence, and these birds, originating in the arid regions of the middle east, have evidently learned the benefits of vitamins and trace elements to be found in seaweed.

Originally a bird of Asiatic regions, the collared dove has adapted to life in urban Britain, becoming a commensal of man, breeding in gardens and feeding on his surplus.

All birds need to bath regularly to keep their plumage in good condition, but collared doves seem to enjoy bathing more than others. Not only do they waddle into water and splash about like other birds but also, more than any other that I have seen, they pay particular attention to the underwing. With steady rain falling, I saw one standing in water up to its belly and holding alternate wings high in the air, evidently allowing the rain to fall on its 'armpits'. At times it was almost lying over on its back in the water. This continued for some three minutes, each side being exposed for about twenty seconds at a time, until the saturated bird flew up to a nearby wall. I have seen them many times, lying on their sides in pouring rain with a wing held high to allow the axillaries, the 'armpit' feathers to become saturated, then they change sides and treat the other wing. They will also rub their underwings in grass wet with dew for the same result. I have seen one doing this within a couple of metres of a pond where other species were splashing about in joyous abandon. I wonder if this is an adaptation to sparse rainfall in their area of origin, enabling them to exploit the slightest dews.

Not all wildlife watching is done during the day. Indeed many of our animals are nocturnal and rarely seen at any other time. The most noticeable decline in nocturnal, or at least crepuscular, species is among the bats. The pipistrelle was very common in my youth, and when we came out after tea on summer evenings, to increase our knowledge of wildlife by playing hopscotch or doctors and nurses until dusk, the little bats emerged and frightened the girls, who were quite convinced they would get in their hair and suck all the blood out of their heads. (So was I.) It was quite usual to see a dozen pipistrelles flying about at the end of our street. Even until the 1970s we saw the large noctules flying about the tower of the church of St John in the Fields. They flew high, with a characteristic wing motion, unlike our other large bat, the greater horseshoe, which flew low among trees and shrubs, and could be seen in car headlights.

While driving along the northern boundary of Clowance estate I was sorry to strike one of these, which became entangled in the car's radiator grill. At that time it was unusual to see a bat in the hand, for there were no bat hospitals or rescue centres, and I marvelled at the structure of the delicate membranes and bones that formed the wings. I couldn't bear to throw it in the dustbin and went to the chemist for some formalin which I injected into the body before stretching it out on a board. It didn't last very long but, while it did, I gave it pride of place. One other bat I examined closely, and the only time I identified the species for sure, was a long-eared bat that became entangled in my mist net when I was trapping birds for ringing at Porthgwarra. Isn't it amazing how wary we are of getting bitten by them? Well they do carry rabies, so we're told, and they migrate, so it was with some circumspection that I untangled and released it. The point here is that any opportunity to learn about our wild things, especially those that we see but rarely, should not be missed.

In Afghanistan, I saw a villager kill a snake that my son later identified from photographs as a harmless javelin sand boa. I cut the snake open and inside was a rat, which I also cut open. The rat was full of grain stolen from the villager's store, so I tried to convince him that the snake was his friend. Prejudice against them is universal, so no doubt he went on killing every snake he saw. Similarly, when I saw a farmer shooting jackdaws in a potato field at Porthleven, I picked up a dead one and cut open its gizzard to show him that inside was not potato but leatherjackets which had indeed been eating the spuds. The birds spent some time with heads low, looking at the ground before digging into the soil, and I was convinced they were waiting for some movement from the grub to indicate where to dig.

On June nights, when there is enough breeze to waft away the human scent, it is great fun to go badger-watching. Despite the fact that few people have ever seen a live one, they are very common in the area in which I live. Although I personally don't know just how many setts there are, and the information is regarded as a state secret by MAFF (as DEFRA will always be to me) they number in hundreds and it is probable that, wherever you might be in Cornwall, you are not more than half a mile from one. Badger tracks are everywhere, and the tell-tale latrines and freshly excavated earth indicate recent occupation. Some setts have been used for hundreds of years, and the excavated earth amounts to cartloads, with several entrances and tracks like highways leading to them. The best setts to watch are those near a footpath, preferably one that actually straddles a path, for then the animals are used to human smells and more likely to emerge early. Stay downwind and keep still. As it gets dark or, with the nights so short, earlier if you are lucky, the old ones come out and sniff the air. If all is clear the cubs follow. By now they will be well grown and will soon wander off to scavenge away from the sett. To see them playing at the entrance it is better to watch in May, when they first emerge.

As part of the week's activities, I used to take visitors to our guesthouse on a badger-watching expedition if they were interested. Not everyone wants to lie about in wet bracken for hours in the hope of seeing the animals when their favourite programme is on the telly. Fair enough, but what surprised me was the number of people who were terrified of the dark. A little rustle, from a mouse or a hedgehog, or a nightjar churring, turned grown men and women to jelly. Sometimes, ten minutes was more than enough of this horror and torches came on, along with enough chatter to keep the badgers underground for weeks. Others, however, were thrilled to bits and thought it the best experience of their holiday. I must admit to being a bit scared myself on one occasion when a friend and I were lying flat and silent downwind of a sett when an old boar (by its size) came ambling right up to us with, apparently, no intention of giving way to a couple of dead humans. Badgers have a formidable set of teeth. It was just a couple of metres away before it sniffed us and bolted off in the other direction. On reflection, has anyone ever been bitten by an unprovoked badger? I think not, but at the same sett we were nearly trampled by horses spooked by suddenly finding us in lying in their way in the pitch dark. Maybe the telly addicts have a point.

Less hazardous but equally thrilling is to go out on summer nights and listen for nightjars. They favour moorland and the bracken-covered slopes of hills. Usually the first churrings are heard, and the dim shapes discerned, when it is just a bit too dark to see them well. We hear the sharp 'keriik' and the wings clapped together as the males display over their territories. Numbers have declined but

Some sett entrances are huge. Fresh excavations indicate current usage, with bedding replenished and regularly brought out for airing.

they are still thinly distributed in suitable habitat throughout Penwith and Kerrier. Well known sites are on the Lizard and at Carn Galver, where you can park by Bosigran engine house and listen just before dusk. On some nights they emerge early and will fly around your head before the sun has fully set, a wonderful experience. While it is not always advisable to disclose exact locations for vulnerable species, there are some sites so well watched that it's as well to let them be generally known, for this not only enables everyone interested to share the experience but can also ensure that the site is protected from harm.

There was a time when badger and nightjar watching, often at the same time, also meant encounters with little owls. They were common in the 1950s but seem now to have disappeared. The last one I saw was at St Levan, ten years ago. The species was introduced, so their hold may always have been tenuous, but that does not apply to our other breeding owls, the barn and tawny. They are still with us, despite the almost total loss of man-made breeding sites for the barn owl and, I think, too much disturbance and rat poison for the tawny. Barn owls are the most frequently seen, usually nothing more than a ghostly shape in car headlights, while the tawny is the most frequently heard, when they begin calling in autumn. Of the other owls, the short-eared are regular winter visitors and should be looked for late on windless afternoons when they may be seen hunting over the moors for voles. Some years they are quite common (for owls) and the most reported, yet in others they are quite scarce. Their presence here depends upon the success of their breeding season and the abundance of food.

In about 1950 I acquired my first simple camera. It was utterly hopeless for taking photographs of birds, yet I had a go at photographing a young cuckoo out of a rock pipit's nest on St Ives Island and a young owl in an old crow's nest in a tree at Carbis Bay. I climbed up and snapped it while the owl looked at me in astonishment. I wasn't quite sure what kind of owl it was, for tawnies do not normally breed in open nests and neither do barn owls. Short-eared owls are only here in winter, and breed on the ground. Little owls breed in holes and were too small. That left long-eared, which didn't breed in west Cornwall and had been proven to breed in the whole county only three times. The photo was more or less forgotten until 2000 when I found a long-eared owl at a site in Penwith in summer and looked it up in my newer reference books. The young depicted here were, I recalled, like the one in my old photograph. After much searching and rummaging I found it and, sure enough, the owlet was, by its distinct dark facial mask, undoubtedly a long-eared owl, the one and only breeding record for west Cornwall. I wish I had put a precise date on the photo.

This old snap of a young long-eared owl was taken when I climbed to the top of a tree at Longstone plantation, now the cemetery, at Carbis Bay to see what was in the nest. It took me fifty years to identify the species from the dark face-mask, and prove the only breeding record for west Cornwall. Very lax of me.

The 2000 bird was not proven to breed, and foot and mouth disease prevented me from checking the site in 2001. It is incredible that, with hundreds of bird-watchers and naturalists about, we still know so little about the distribution of so many species.

When observing wildlife in general there is always some doubt whether we should go stomping through the countryside, in order to cover as much ground as possible, or sit quietly and wait to see what emerges. Wildlife watchers have been divided between those who rush about from place to place and those who sit and wait. Unless we cover the ground, some say, we will never learn new areas or discover what is in them, and a long walk over the moors or along the cliffs is always productive. The same route is never the same twice; the changing seasons see to that, as does the time of day. The long shadows of early morning and the western sky at sunset light our view with ever-changing intensity, and each new brow surmounted or valley entered is as entering a new world of discovery. Others maintain that the only way to watch is to sit and keep one's eyes open. Sitting about for long periods in the middle of winter may be only for the dedicated but during the rest of the year it is another matter. By sitting quietly, we are far more likely to see animals doing something other than scurrying away in fright. In 2001, while watching peregrines, I caught movement out of the corner of my eye and, by slowly turning my head, was delighted to see a stoat just a few metres away. It ran about among a group of boulders, appearing and disappearing for several minutes before going to ground. There is great satisfaction in knowing that we have been so close to some wild and wary creature completely undetected.

Some years go I had a similar experience with a stoat, but the remains of that one appeared on a buzzard's larder a few days later. On another occasion, while driving along a country lane, I saw a stoat dragging a rabbit along the verge and stopped my car to watch through the wing mirror. It was as much as the stoat could manage but, by pulling hard with the rabbit over its shoulder, it came up right beside me, where it attempted to drag the rabbit down a hole. The rabbit was far too large, and only the head went in, leaving me to watch the rear end quivering as, no doubt, the front end was fed to a brood of young stoats somewhere underground. All this emphasises the importance of keeping quiet with eyes open if we are to see more than a fleeting glimpse of wildlife; that is all I've ever had of a weasel, the stoat's little cousin, except for a female lying in a gin-trap with a tiny young one trying to suckle from the dead body. Thankfully, such sights are no longer seen since the banning of these cruel and indiscriminate traps some years ago.

Over the years I have spent many hours sitting quietly watching buzzards, for instance, and have seen much that a casual walker, or one intent on rapid progress, would inadvertently overlook. Buzzards are something of a Cornish speciality and worthy of time spent watching them. Like all birds of prey, they have such efficient eyesight that trying to hide from them is almost a waste of time. Unless in a hide, you might as well sit out in the open as lie half concealed behind a bush. They know you are there, have no doubt about it. Buzzards' behaviour is conditional on circumstance, obviously! In the 1930s and 40s, when they were persecuted as vermin, they were so wary that it was almost impossible to get close to one. As far as I am aware, no census of Cornish buzzards was ever undertaken at that time, so it is difficult to make accurate assessment of changes, either in population or behaviour. That they were formerly much rarer is certain. B.H. Ryves, writing in *Bird Life in Cornwall* in 1948 stated that the buzzard 'has now established itself firmly even in the Land's End peninsula where, as recently as 1930, it was very rare'.

Lady's smock, always a delicate bloom, is to be found in damp meadows and streamsides.

That they remained uncommon, and wary, I can verify. At the time of the introduction of myxomatosis, when the rabbit population crashed, I did a census for the Nature Conservancy and found not a single breeding pair in the Penwith peninsula. The birds were there, but there was insufficient food to bring them into breeding condition. Even in those days there were farmers who protected birds of prey, however, and on farms where unmolested they might nest in the same tree for many years. There was a solitary pine tree near Zennor in which there was a buzzards' nest of gigantic proportions, having been added to, spring after spring, for over twenty years. Eventually the tree came down in a gale and the buzzards moved to the cliff. Nowadays, every farmer that I have spoken to is delighted to have a pair of these birds nesting on his land, where they help keep the rabbits under control. In a personal study in the mid-90s I found some 50 pairs in Penwith and they are probably just as densely distributed throughout Cornwall. They must have reached saturation point but are still able to rear two young in good years, as in 2001 when the rabbit population was high, whereas in a leaner year the weaker chick gets eaten by its sibling.

By sitting on some vantage point we can watch these stately birds through their breeding cycle, from the nest-building very early in the spring, and very early in the morning, to the feeding of the young long after they have left the nest, sometimes right through to the end of October. At this time, in an arbitrary area, say Penwith and Kerrier, there are, assuming a successful breeding season, some 200 adults, and let us not exaggerate, 100 young. That equals at least 300 buzzards. The buzzard's individual food requirement has been variously estimated from 100 to 140 grams per day. Let's allow for hard times and say 100 grams. Multiplied by 300 this equals 30 000 grams per day = 30 kgs, times 365 days = 10 950 kilograms of rabbits, voles, reptiles and invertebrates a year on my calculator. Wow! How do they find such quantities? Have you ever tried to find a mouse in field, or an adder or a vole? When we consider that kestrels, owls, foxes, stoats and weasels are all preying on the same populations it just indicates how little we humans see of what is out there. To quote figures from L. Harrison Mathews' *British Mammals* (1952):

The weight of rabbits consigned from railway stations in only three counties of west Wales in 1948 are illuminating. The weight totalled no less than 3320 tons which represents about four and a half million rabbits… In the same year over eight hundred tons of rabbits were shipped from both Devon and Cornwall.

That is over 1 million rabbits exported from Cornwall in one year that made no difference to the overall population.

Returning briefly to springtime, it is worth a visit to some prominent hilltop on fine days in March and early April, when there are thermals rising from the warming ground. Scan the skies and it is not unusual to see 20 buzzards in the air. They display in pairs over the breeding areas, intercepting intruders and wheeling and diving in a series of drops and rises in which they almost loop the loop. I have never seen one actually turn right over, but pretty near. If you are lucky you might see the locking of talons as two birds grasp each other and fall like a whirligig, separating just as it seems they would crash on to the ground. I have only seen this behaviour for a very short time, just prior to egg laying. Buzzards are far less tolerant of their nest site being overlooked than are peregrines, but they are becoming tamer as persecution decreases, even, in one case, nesting in a pine tree in a small garden. There is one nest so low down that it can be seen into from the buses passing close by on the road. At one site, where I like to think the birds have come to know me (probably wishful thinking), I have sat in full view some 200 metres from the nest while they brought in prey for the young. It is on a cliff-top prominence where many walkers pause to admire the view, and the birds have become used to the strange behaviour of humans. They take a variety of prey, and among items on this pair's larder, a site where the prey is prepared for the chicks, I once saw a jackdaw, the remains of rabbits, and two dead adders. They may frequently be seen carrying snakes. While sitting at the head of a valley I saw a buzzard drop on to some small item, which it took to a grass-grown ant heap. When it had finished eating and flown off I went down and found the remains of a toad. Some items are more of a problem and, in October 1994, one I saw at Heamoor had caught a large eel from a ditch. Unlike ospreys and herons, buzzards are not equipped to deal with such slippery customers and after much struggling, with the eel twining itself around the buzzard's legs, the unfortunate creature was swallowed *eight* times, leaving just the tip of its tail showing, and seven times wriggled back up the gullet before being finally subdued. Although territorial in the breeding season, the barriers seem to get broken in autumn, and there was an occasion in Oct 1999 when there were twenty-six sitting in a small ploughed field at Sancreed. They were probably looking for invertebrates, for they will follow the plough in winter, waddling along in the furrows looking for worms.

Summertime brings such an exuberance of wild flowers that any account of them would require several volumes. The most obvious displays, seen along our lanes, occur mainly as a result of the traditional stone walls that we still call hedges. Being raised above ground level the soil dries out quickly and coarse plants, requiring uninterrupted supplies of moisture, tend to be successively eliminated toward the top, leaving the drought-tolerant but more floriferous species to survive over the years. The succession of colour depends also on maintenance, and the finest displays can sometimes follow early trimming, when the dazzling yellows of cat's ear and hawksbeard are intermingled with the powder-blues and pinks of sheepsbit and stonecrop, providing displays we are hard put to equal in the best of gardens. It is also worth getting down on hands and knees in a nice soggy swamp to look among the bog asphodels for the even more delicate specialities such as bog pimpernel and, with luck, the tiny pitcher-like flowers of the insectivorous pale butterwort which, along with that other carnivore, the sundew, may be found in a few sites. Look in permanently damp patches of soil too shallow to support more vigorous competitors.

The urge to place one stone on top of another seems to be an ancient need in man, but I think it might have reached its peak in such works of ephemeral art as this. After watching its painstaking construction, and ignoring the assumption that it was meant to be destroyed by the incoming tide, I sneaked a photo when the builder had gone on his way. My apologies, whoever you are.

In damper hollows marsh ragwort proliferates in some years, to be quite scarce in others. The trampling of cattle allows the first and second colonisers to flourish before being swamped by coarser perennials.

Carn Euny. After thousands of years of human modification, this is still a prime spot for seeing upland species. In 2000 swallows built a nest in the underground chamber.

A newly emerged golden-ringed dragonfly shelters among bracken fronds. As you see, they rest with wings together as they are drying, part of the development on emergence from the lava, which can take a couple of hours, so this is not an infallible way of distinguishing them from damselflies at this stage. An insect of faster-flowing streams than other large dragonflies, the golden-ringed is also one of the largest and certainly the easiest to identify. It wanders far from water when not breeding.

Not all of the water around Cornwall is salt. Our streams abound with life. Pink purslane, one of the less noxious alien plants, grows along the bank, together with water dropwort which can choke a stream.

A fine trout treads water over the gravel. The scouring out of streams by the floods of winter 2002/3 will probably benefit these fish as they require gravelly reaches unchoked by weeds over which to spawn.

Still relatively plentiful in unmodified heaths and scrub, the common lizard is usually seen as a quick blur scurrying away from the unobservant walker. Tread softly if you would see them, especially along the trimmed edges of our coastal paths, where they enjoy sunbathing throughout the warmer months.

No two shores are the same. Here, at Trevail, on the exposed north coast, the bedrock has been worn smooth by the action of the waves rolling boulders during storms. Grazing limpets keep the rocks bare of weed.

A miniature cavern, just 300mm (12ins) high is like a tropical jungle in its luxuriance. Tidal pools and the shady nooks at this level are utterly fascinating for those with an eye for detail.

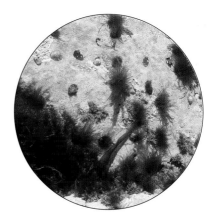

Even at the top of the shore, a world of mystery and tranquillity awaits in the tidal pools at low water.

A sea hare which has come inshore to breed and browse on weed.

This towering granite column near Porthcurnow shows how the various forms of life it supports are adapted to exploit the sequence of exposure and altitude. All the zones, from seaweeds through barnacles right up to the yellow Xanthoria, lichens are clearly defined.

The presence of barnacles and sea anemones indicate that they are covered by every tide and do not dry out.

Summer mists, which can obliterate much of the coast just when we think there is a fine day coming, light the countryside in soft glows on summer afternoons.

When distant views are obscured we can turn to closer things, often overlooked in the general view. Here, yellow bartsia grows amid cow parsley umbels and rushes.

The valley of the Hayle river, between St Erth and Relubbus. One of the most interesting, yet least-known, wildlife areas in Cornwall, it has the most diverse of habitats in such a confined space, varying from mature woodland to wet and dry fields, scrub, dry banks, willows, reedbeds, marshes, ponds and the river itself. There are many interesting plants and insects, and the author has recorded 84 species of bird with 48 breeding, in a 3-mile walk. There are otters in the river system and probably a remnant population of the near-extinct water-vole, for I saw one here in 2002. Such an area requires and deserves careful management if it is to retain its special character. The white-flowered dropwort (seen right) might eventually obliterate the reeds, with consequent loss of a thriving reed warbler colony. Nothing is static in nature.

Old industry was on a comparatively small scale so that abandoned workings, as at this disused quarry, soon recuperated to become important wildlife habitats in their own right. Barn owls breed in the crevices of this miniature cliff blasted from the solid rock.

A rare sight nowadays, an unsprayed boggy field, with a fine example of marsh thistle among the buttercups. Elderflowers glow white in the distance.

Also a rare sight, these young elm trees were photographed in the 1970s, before they were devastated by disease. They are now beginning to regenerate from the old stools. Although these trees shed thousands of seeds each year, I have never seen a seedling elm, and wonder if every single one in Cornwall was planted from cuttings or suckers.

Two dunlin and an American pectoral sandpiper at Drift Reservoir. Such areas are at their best for wading birds after a dry summer, when falling water levels expose the muddy banks.

Years of drought reveal the tree stumps and old farm walls that were covered by Drift Reservoir.

The lane to Treveal Cove, near Zennor, in high summer, is a succession of beautiful wild flowers when there is no spraying.

This stretch of coast is the reward for those who make the walk from St Ives to Zennor,
at least for some people, some of the time. On the last occasion I did so we had rain
all the way, but it is still a magnificent scene on a day such as this.

Another community of wild flowers, with purple loosestrife, meadowsweet, sea carrot and hemp agrimony against a background of the geological Site of Special Scientific Interest at Porthmeor Cove. This is also a fishing ground for grey seals.

Inset: *Normally a plant of boggy ground, purple loosestrife may also be found thriving in rock crevices that are constantly watered by drainage from above.*

The tall mine stacks are regularly used by buzzards, ravens, and kestrels for lookout sites. They are sometimes occupied by nesting jackdaws but a well-built one will have few holes or ledges inside.

Rubble has been strewn over the ground at Geevor to cover up the arsenic, as if anybody was likely to lick it off the rocks. See how nature is already beginning to clothe the area in heather. Or was seed scattered? What a sight it will be in ten years' time if left alone.

Always one of the first colonisers after a burnout or a soil disturbance, these foxgloves at Tehidy sprang up where a fallen tree had exposed the soil and let in the sunlight.

A feast of nectar for this gate-keeper butterfly on wild thyme. The larval food plants of this, and most of the brown butterflies, are Poa and other abundant grasses, so the numbers fluctuate as a result of adverse weather at critical times.

Sea asters grow from solid rock, it appears, and also favour the scree of shredded slate and granite. The blooms look far too tender for such a harsh environment.

Wild thyme and sea carrot on the edge of the sea. Such a habitat was once populated by large blue butterflies.

Something of a rarity, found in only a few favoured sites, dyer's greenweed, Genista tinctoria as the name implies was formerly used as a strong dye. It forms low clusters amongst short turf and is easily overlooked as being gorse or broom.

Montbretia is an attractive, but insidious, menace which spreads inexorably, wiping out all before it with those tight-clustered corms.

Inset: *Orchids can be difficult to identify for they are very variable and often hybridise with each other. This one, with the help of books and other experts, was identified as southern marsh orchid in 1987. A fine specimen, it was growing in a boggy patch with no other orchids in the vicinity.*

Main: *Fifteen years later the same plant produced 43 spikes of magnificent flowers.*

Bee orchid and grass vetchling. Two rarities in Cornwall, normally requiring more alkaline soil than we can offer. A thriving mixed colony of both established itself after major roadworks disturbed the ground.

The same view, seen with different lights or states of the tide as the seasons progress, offers constant new opportunity to the photographer. This place is vaguely marked on the OS map as Brandys, which I like to think is a corruption of the Kernewek Bran Ty, (Raven's House), for they do breed nearby. There are three huge columns of rock here which, when seen from the sea,

are prominent landmarks. They were pointed out to me in my fishing days as the Three Brazen Men, evidently yet another corruption of Kernewek, this time of Try Brassa Meyn (the three big, or biggest, stones). Nearly every place name with men or man in it is from meyn (or maen), such as the several Man-o'-war rocks for meyn an mor (rock of, or in, the sea).

The uniform greens of summer perhaps make less interesting pictures but the groundswell leaves a tell-tale pattern of currents along the coast. It is in such currents, and where two tides meet, that the basking sharks find the richest plankton, so here is a good place to look for them in early summer.

The streams that run off the moors and trickle through the boulders of the various coves have been deepened by centuries of tin streaming but are of interest to wildlife all along their lengths. Here, damselflies glitter their reds and blues among the blanketing green vegetation of late summer.

Red mine-spoil, claggy and polluted, takes a long time to be colonised by any plants.

KYNYAF

AUTUMN

The world is full of colour!
'Tis autumn once again
And leaves of gold and crimson
Are lying in the lane.

Colour Adeline White

And now, all too soon, the shortening days bring on the season of mists and (wait for it) blackberry and apple pie. The autumn leaves are short-lasting in Cornwall. As soon as the colours begin to glow in the lowering sunshine an equinoxial gale will, as like as not, whip them off to carpet the woodland floors in a rustling pile. In years when the gales are few, or are of little strength, and the rain delays its deluge, the leaves hang on in sheltered valleys and the lee sides of woods. It is then that the beeches and alders and acers are at their finest, but the best of our colour is from other sources. First, the three species of heather on the moors, the bell heather, *Erica cinerea*, followed by ling, *Calluna vulgaris*, and cross-leaved heath, *Erica tetralix*. The bell heather is the brightest purple and the first to flower, beginning in June, and is most tolerant of dry conditions, often growing on banks and dry walls where the ling does not compete. The cross-leaved heath, with leaves of silvery grey and flowers of pink, grows best in damp, even boggy situations, as long as there is full, uninterrupted sunshine. No heather will tolerate shade. On the Lizard there also grows the Cornish heath, *Erica vagans*, which has wide variations and has parented many a garden variety with fancy names. A few clumps of white ling may be found, but usually it is in shades of dull purple and relies on mass carpeting for full effect. For about three weeks in September all four are in flower together and the

Cherry trees that delighted us in spring put on an equally spectacular show in autumn.

sparse soils of cliff top and moorland glow with dazzling colour. The colour is even more spectacular when the brilliant, contrasting yellow of the dwarf western gorse emerges, lasting into October. Around the same time the bracken turns and the slopes of the hills become covered in a russet glow in the sunshine. Higher up, where the soil is too shallow for bracken, and too poor even for the heathers, we find the swathes of pale yellow moor grass contrasting with the dark greens of rabbit-nibbled turf among the grey granite carns. The countryside is now at its best in showing off its colour and, on those days when the skies are of that particularly intense blue, which they can be in autumn, and when, after a shower of rain, dark-centred clouds over an indigo sea intensify the contrasts even up into the heavens, we are fully reconciled to the loss of summer for another year.

Autumn is when the migration of birds is most evident. Whereas small land birds move mostly at night, seabirds are on the move at all times and are to be seen moving off our coasts throughout daylight hours when the weather is right. The numbers seen inshore depend entirely on the weather; on some days, even though they might be passing in thousands over the horizon, hardly any are seen from land but with an onshore wind and a drop of rain they pass close in. The largest numbers occur in late summer and autumn, when the commuting adults are joined by young ones making their first flights, and huge numbers are occasionally recorded. The most concentrated passage of shearwaters I have seen occurred on 13 September 2001, off Levant. In excess of 200 per minute were passing from 1500hrs to 1800hrs, when I left. 200 x 60 = 12 000 an hour, for three-and-a-half hours = 42 000. Other watchers recorded them in similar numbers from Godrevy and Pendeen for most of the day. A spectacular sight, they were like a continuous swarm of bees moving west. At the same time there were more than 50 gannets per minute on the move, as well as less numerous skuas, fulmars, and rare sabines gulls. It is not exceptional to see over 100 000 birds go by our headlands in a day's watch.

As far as is known, Manx shearwaters have never bred on the mainland of Cornwall. They breed on the Isles of Scilly and may be seen passing the headlands of west Cornwall throughout the summer when they are commuting from the breeding-islands fringing the Atlantic and Irish seas to feeding-grounds as far south as Biscay. Apart from being on a breeding island at night, when the incoming birds will land at your feet, you are unlikely to experience close encounters of the shearwater kind, for they will not venture ashore in

At Perranporth boating pool this red-necked phalarope stayed for several days, delighting all who saw it at such close quarters. Birds of the red-necked species are less frequent than the greys, but the latter are usually seen only as small white dots flying by a headland in a storm.

daylight. There was one unusually close encounter on the island of St Agnes in the 1960s when there were all of six birders over there where now there would be 600. They were invited to dinner one windy night by Gordon George and his wife, Ruth. Her specialty was 'bird-watchers' cake', a delicious stodge of which she baked huge quantities and fed to hungry birders when they passed her door. On the night of the dinner, a huge meal, all were sitting at the table yarning as the wind and rain swirled around the island, when suddenly there was an explosion of splintering glass flying all over the room. It took a few moments to recover the senses and realise that a Manx shearwater had crashed through the window and landed on the table among the remains of the meal. As they come ashore only at night, it is a mystery why it made for the light from the window. Once, after another gale, a storm petrel, was found grounded in the Digey, St Ives. It was brought to me but I could see nothing wrong with it. It just refused to fly. Then I realised the reason and took it to the shore at night, when it ruffled its feathers and flew off into the darkness. It seems these petrels are completely inhibited from flying to or from the shore in daylight.

Mid-October sees the first of the migrant thrushes dropping in, but it is usually in the last few days and the first week in November when the majority arrive. They come from far and wide, redwings and fieldfares from Scandinavia, song thrushes from there also, and those dark individuals we see are probably from Iceland, as are some of the redwings. They are recognised taxonomically as distinct races, although identification in the field is a matter of some speculation. They are always hungry after their long flights and depend on the berry crop to replenish the energy lost on the journey. In a good year, which is one in which the weather was fine during the time of blossom, the county is aglow with the crop of red berries on the hawthorn. This little tree is more abundant here than anywhere else I have been, and is characteristic of the landscape, both around the cultivated fields and on the fringes of the moors and woods. In sheltered valleys where it is left to grow it forms low woods of thick boles and spreading canopy. On the moors and exposed Cornish hedges, solitary specimens defy the elements in surviving with gnarled trunks, contorted branches and twigs that succumb to the gales and lean away to shelter the buds through the winter. It is, in fact, only the early gales that cause this distortion. When the buds are enclosed in their winter sheaths they are safe from both wind and frost, but when wind-blown salt is driven by the autumn gales and spreads inland the open buds are burnt away and the growth of the following year is lost. Only those sheltered by the tree's own canopy, with their backs to the wind, survive to grow another year. The haws are eaten by all the thrushes, kernel and all, by wood-pigeons and, naturally, by hawfinches, though you'll be very lucky to see one in Cornwall. The migrants, flying high as they reach the coast, will spy the haws from afar and descend in hordes to gorge themselves on nature's bounty. In years of dearth they are forced to look elsewhere for sustenance and descend on the upland fields where they will spend most of the winter eating invertebrates.

Even more vulnerable to the vagaries of our fickle climate than haws are the sloes. Blackthorns are not consistent in their flowering time. Cold, dark winters will delay them until April. When they put out their white blossom in March, perhaps deceived by a warm winter, they do not always set fruit if the weather is dull and no bees fly. The blossom is almost ethereal in its delicacy and duration, so a period of clement weather is even more crucial than with the hawthorn. In some years the sloe blossom is hardly noticed, so brief is its appearance, and heavy rain reduces the pristine whiteness to a soggy brown mass in hours, whereas in a fine spell the delicate white flowers set against the black stems brighten our walks along the narrow lanes. Fortunately, the variation between the microclimates of exposed cliff and sheltered vale ensure that blossoming time is extended and never is all completely lost. Sloes, like all berries, are eaten by birds but, being too big for many to swallow, are often left to shrivel on the branch if there is plenty choice elsewhere.

Smaller birds will settle in weedy fields, where the berries of black nightshade, so poisonous to us, are eagerly eaten with impunity. It is the same with the red arils, that most of us are happy to call berries, surrounding the seeds of yew. Red is the colour usually associated with berries, yet many are black. Bramble, the nightshades, sloes, privet, elder and ivy are all black and glossy. There must be some advantage in this, but I know not what. Perhaps they are invisible until ripe, when the gloss on the skin makes them conspicuous as the sun shines or they are wetted by dew.

We should encourage native species in our gardens if we have the space, but, of all the berries, wild and cultivated, native and alien, I know of no others which are devoured so avidly as the black berries of the common myrtle, *Myrtus communis*. This shrub, or small tree, with cinnamon bark and white flowers in late summer, is a native of the Mediterranean and my gardening books say it is half-hardy and that the flowers are 'sometimes' followed by black fruits.

Half-hardy it may be and in hard winters is severely cut back, even in west Cornwall, yet, in my garden at least, the berry crop is reliable and prolific year on year. Birds just love it. I have recorded 7 blackbirds, 2 song thrushes, 3 species of tit and a firecrest all feeding at one time in a small tree of about 4 metres in height. The tiny firecrest, just about managing to eat a whole berry without choking itself to death, evidently thought the risk was worth it. Altogether I have recorded some 20 species in this one tree. Anyone wishing to encourage berry-eating birds to their garden in our mild Cornish climate would be well advised to plant one. We see more of our gardens than any other area of the world, I suppose, so by making them wildlife-friendly we are likely to see more birds and beasts than anywhere else.

A tree which is still small, though larger than the myrtle, is the *Cornus capitata* (or is it now called *Dendrobenthamia capitata*), Bentham's Cornel. This has large pale-yellow or white flowers (actually they are bracts surrounding an insignificant flower), which alone make the tree worth growing in a garden large enough to take it. The flowers are followed, again depending on the exact time of flowering, but usually in October and November, by large strawberry-like fruits which the birds adore. This also is frost- to half-hardy but I know of one in St Ives, which has seen all of fifty winters and is still thriving. Both this and the myrtle throw plenty of germinating seedlings after the fruit has passed through the gut of a bird, so are readily replaced or increased to pass on to fellow bird-feeding gardeners. One popular berry-bearer, which the birds leave untouched until everything else has been consumed, is the firethorn, *Pyracantha atlantioides*, which can be overloaded with berries if grown in sun. In my garden they last through December in most years.

A male blackbird gorges itself on black myrtle berries.

The great autumn feast for many species is to be found in the oak tree. Its prolific crop of leaves holds a myriad of insects until quite late in the year, while its fissured bark shelters many spiders and beetles throughout the winter. In October the jays, so secretive for much of the year when their presence is only detected by their raucous, screeching call-notes, become conspicuous as they fly over town and country searching for acorn-bearing oaks. Having found a crop they fly from source to secret hiding places where hundreds of acorns are stored for the winter. Often working in pairs, for security I think, for these colourful crows are as crafty as any magpie, they fly high above our heads, alighting on oak trees in town parks and gardens where normally they are too wary to visit. When the leaves are fallen, there is still a crop of acorns to be gathered from the evergreen holm oaks which were so popularly planted early in the last century. These trees are now fully mature and produce large numbers of acorns that often fall on town pavements and are crushed underfoot. I have seen flocks of rooks and jackdaws descend upon one of these huge trees day after day until every acorn was either eaten or taken away and hidden. Those forgotten or undiscovered by mice and voles germinate to spread the oak trees over new ground. The young oaks appearing on the eastern slopes of Trencrom Hill were probably planted in this manner. Were it not for fires many of our hills would eventually be afforested.

After a dry summer, followed by rain in autumn, be prepared to go off on fungus forays. That simply means going for a walk and, as in all wildlife walks, keeping your eyes open, this time for fungus and mushrooms. These are one and the same thing although the conventional distinction in Britain is that mushrooms are good to eat and fungus poisonous. They grow almost everywhere, from dry rot under floors, if there is a spot of unrepaired damp, to the tops of mountains. On Bodmin Moor you will find the brightly-coloured wax caps among short, sheep- or rabbit-nibbled, turf, and the small black candelabra fungus with white sporing bodies which send clouds like fine white powder into the air when touched. Here you might find also the round earth balls and puffballs which do indeed send out clouds of brown spores when gently squeezed. In pasture, especially where there have been horses it is said, and I have to agree with this, the white round spheres of field and horse mushrooms appear in autumn too. They make the bought ones taste like globes of white polystyrene by comparison. If you are lucky you might find the huge parasol, one of which is a feast, or even the giant puffball, which will feed a family. I have found the latter growing in pasture among cattle near Sancreed, but never a fresh one, although a friend once gave me half of one, which was fried in butter and devoured with relish.

Many fungi species are dependent on specific hosts. Some are found only under pine, some only under birch for example, but many are more catholic and parasitise, for parasites most of them are, a variety of hosts. Many are saprophytes and grown only on dead timber or rotting leaves; some grow only as parasites on other fungi. Many of the more conspicuous fungi grow on or near the ground as parasites on trees so a fungus foray through the woods will probably be the most productive in your search. Trevaylor Woods near Penzance or Pendarves Wood at Camborne are good places to look, as indeed is any wood with established and, especially, rotting timber. The walk along the shores of Loe Pool at Helston has always been productive too. Here again,

Carrion crows hang about at the entrance to rabbit burrows. I don't know what they can be waiting for but this behaviour is quite common. They might be waiting for an unsuspecting baby rabbit to emerge.

a few basic names need learning, but some are easily identified down to family and genus, although difficult as to species. The colourful *Russulas* with red or green caps, and the *Boletes* with tiny holes instead of gills underneath, are perhaps the first for beginners to look for. Up the trunks you will find the tough bracket fungi, like oval shelves jammed into the trunk, with concentric rings of yellow and brown above and thousands of spore-releasing pores below. In some woods, growing on birch or pine, are found the brilliant red-with-white-spots fly agarics. They are beautiful but poisonous and not to be eaten. I have not found them in Cornwall's woods but am told they do occur. I have seen them in urban gardens, however, usually with a gnome or a Cornish pisky sitting atop. Go out and enjoy identifying your mushrooms with a good field guide, preferably leaving them growing for others to enjoy, but I would advise against eating any of them, for some are deadly poisonous and not worth the risk. I would especially advise that you do not collect any of the really delicious ones if you see me following you!

A characteristic magpie's nest, with its thick dome of thorns, a bit overdone in this case. Magpies build their nests very early, often before the leaves are on the trees, either high up or in thick cover such as a prickly sloe or hawthorn.

In autumn you will see gatherings of magpies. It is not exceptional to see flocks of 20 or more during the day, and double that when they gather to roost. Thirty or more roost in one *Cupressus macrocarpa* tree in the centre of Penzance. These social gatherings are undertaken with much chattering and squabbling and may be where the young of the year sort out their place amongst the established pecking order and find mates for the following spring. They defend breeding territories, seeing off any intruders, but otherwise are as sociable as any other crows. The old saw that one rook is a crow and a flock of crows are rooks is best ignored. Crows gather on flat fields and the open mud of estuaries in autumn and winter when they hold what used to be called 'parliaments'. They can be seen all bowing and cawing to each other as they strut about, like pompous lawyers in their black gowns, when suddenly they turn on one individual and beat the stuffing out of it. It seems lucky to escape with its life and one can but wonder what misdemeanour warranted such punishment. It is true that rooks are nearly always in flocks, but they may be seen alone and some have learned to exploit the generosity of man. More accurately, they exploit the generosity of woman, who is more likely to give away crumbs and unwanted ends of pasties. These birds have learned to wait on people eating in cars at service stations and car parks at beauty spots, as at Marazion, behaviour that the wary magpie has yet to develop.

I have a grudging admiration for magpies. As a schoolboy I worked on a farm. We were allowed time off from lessons as part of the war effort, and I was upset to see the farmer take a shotgun and blast the nests of these beautiful birds out of the hawthorns as 'vermin'. He did the same to carrion crows, ravens, buzzards and anything else with hooked bills and claws. All these were considered to kill chickens, which were all free-range in those days, and sheep. Later, I kept free-range chickens in a valley where there were all of these terrible predators and never lost a thing except for a few eggs that magpies stole from inside the chicken house, and a goose that I saw being dragged away by a fox. Had I a shotgun I would have shot both magpie and fox for, once they acquire a taste for the easy pickings of eggs and fat hens, any individual will come back for more. They will go a long way to get them, for I have seen a fox take two hens to its den of cubs miles from any poultry pens. All these predators will wait for the placenta of sheep. Whether they attack healthy lambs is a matter of some controversy. I have never seen any Cornish predator interested in a live lamb but once they see the opportunity of attacking a still-born or sickly individual, then they might learn from that and start attacking healthy animals.

While we should not condemn predators on circumstantial evidence, the case against the magpie is proven, in my opinion. In that same valley there were three pairs of mistle thrushes that never reared a brood in the fourteen years I lived there. The magpies predated every nest, despite me despatching the one that had learned to steal hen's eggs. It's true that mistle thrushes are hardly the cleverest in concealing their nests, building as they often do on a bare exposed branch or fork in an ash tree, but magpies will search through the trees and bushes on a deliberate nest-plundering foray and take every fledgling they can find. This is the more marked in suburban gardens where the magpies themselves have no predators.

The domestic cat, which is the most active predator we have in our urbanised world, is no match for the magpie. One of our cats was once bringing a vole across the fields to show us how clever a cat she was, and to leave the entrails where we would step on them in our bare feet. Two magpies had other ideas, for a fat vole makes a good snack for two black-and-white brigands to share. In a combined operation they flew towards the enemy, one landing a few feet in front of the cat, the other, unseen, a few feet behind. The front one danced enticingly before the crouching cat, who had to decide whether it was better to hang on to the small vole or go for the more satisfying meal of a magpie. While she crouched in indecision the second bird crept quietly up behind it and jabbed its beak into the cat's nether quarters, causing her to leap about and rush at the second magpie, still holding on to the vole. Then the first magpie flew in and also pecked the cat on the backside. This went on, one bird after the other using diversionary tactics, while the other came in to the attack with a sharp peck on the rump, until the cat finally lost its cool and rushed at the magpie in front of it, dropping the vole in its anger. The bird bounced out of harm's way, while the one behind flew in, picked up the vole, and they made off together, leaving the cat twitching its tail in fury.

A magpie I reared became a bit of a local character in St Ives. It was free-flying, and came back home every night until it felt the call of the wild and went off to live a more natural life. That bird's propensity for thieving was in true magpie tradition. It would steal anything, preferring leather and shiny objects, such as money, and once came in through my bedroom window and stole my wallet. I looked out and saw him hide it on a shelf in the cellar. I had to pretend I had not seen it, for he watched me approach the hiding place, and I had to rush for it or Skipper, as I named him, would have carried off my wallet and week's wages, never to be seen again. He once brought back somebody's purse full of small change, but I felt it expedient to keep quiet about that at the time for fear I might be accused of training him as a professional thief!

He was mischievous too, and his favourite prank was to fly into a hotel's dining room just before dinner, when the tables were beautifully laid with cutlery and vases of flowers. Beginning at one end he would hop up the tables, throwing the cutlery overboard and upsetting vases of flowers until the dining-room was just a scene of utter, saturated devastation, after which act of vandalism he would fly off with a spoon or sugar tongs. I had some flack from the hotel manager over that! I was also in trouble when he went to the Co-op milk crates and pulled off all the shiny silver bottle tops. All this was despite a recent statement in a national bird protection society's magazine stating that magpies' propensity for thieving bright objects is a myth. Signor Rossini, turn in your grave! He also was unafraid of cats and would creep up on any he found sleeping in the sun and jab them in the rump before flying off with a triumphant cackle. Dogs were no threat either. On the putting green at Porthminster, Skipper often dropped in for a sip of water from a dripping tap, and once a greyhound went bounding after him. Completely unfazed, the bird flew a few inches in front of the dog, out of jaw's reach, up and down the green looking back at its pursuer, until the dog collapsed exhausted in a panting heap.

He loved a drop of beer and used to call in at the British Legion to scrounge a quick sip on the way home. On one occasion he was so drunk he flew in like a falling leaf, swerving from side to side, and I had to put him on the end of his perch where he leaned against the wall and fell into deep, intoxicated sleep. At this time I read a letter in the local newspaper from a man up country asking if anyone could send him a grass snake, as he had seen one while stationed here during the war. I wrote and explained that there were no grass snakes here and he had probably seen slow-worms. He asked me to send him one. I went to the railway bridge on Porthminster Hill where I knew slow-worms hid among the grass. I found two and had one in each hand as some tourists were approaching, and a magpie flew over. Thinking that the bird might just be Skipper I called its name. The bird halted in its flight as the people came towards me. It came down with a glide and settled on my shoulder. A small boy in the party gazed wide-eyed at me with open mouth and drooping jaw.

'Ee,' he said, in his drawling Yorkshire accent, 'Did y' see tha' fella? He 'as 'andfuls of snakes and charms birds out o't sky.'

They passed on the other side of the lane, as if in the presence of none other than a reincarnation St Francis of Assisi himself!

A woodchat shrike. This species, only a stray migrant in Britain and always rare, has been recorded in Cornwall on some 80 occasions in the past fifty years.

In the wider world magpies have their place and predators do not normally control their prey, rather the converse, but in the confines of gardens they wield an unnatural power of predation and, in mine at any rate, are not welcome. When I see them eating fledglings alive I wish I could call on my old farmer friend and his shotgun.

Adders, on the other hand, I would never kill. Indeed, it is now illegal to do so. It is unlikely that a prosecution would be brought against anyone for kill one in self-defence but, having handled many adders in my foolish youth and being aware of the favourite sunbathing spots of several, I can assure you that they are not going to attack anybody except in their own self-defence. Your dog, quietly running along ahead, is the most likely casualty. A couple of years back, I was following a friend down a heather-covered slope of the cliff near Gurnard's Head. As he raised his foot, I saw he had just stepped on an adder. The soft vegetation had prevented any injury to the snake and my friend went on unaware.

'You've just stepped on an adder,' I said.

My friend, who is as aware of the benign temperament of adders as I, turned and, where many would have leapt away in fright, leaned over and said to the serpent, 'Aw, sorry, old pal. Didn' mean step on ee.' (He is a Camborne man.) I could have sworn that the adder, as it slithered off, hissed something like, 'I wishhhhhh you would look where you're shhhhhhtepping.' Maybe not!

Another friend has had a very large female in her vegetable garden for four years and she showed it to me, curled up in a seed tray. It probably reduces the numbers of field mice that wreak havoc with her strawberries. Adders are now protected because, like everything else, they are in decline. There used to be dozens of them along the railway embankments between St Ives and St Erth, and all over the open ground at Worvas Hill, now overgrown and shaded into sterility by rhododendron. Along the sunny cliffs of the south coast they still survive in good numbers. Preferring sunny banks on the edge of rough ground where they can hunt for food, they are less often found on the hedges between two cultivated fields. They are so wary as to be difficult to watch and, when found, they are either basking in the sun and immobile or slithering off for fear of meeting a similar fate to the one at Gurnard's Head. If you come across one, be very quiet, for a footfall or loud voice will send it off. If undisturbed they return to the same sunbathing spot every day and, if you are lucky, you can see two or three entwined together.

At Porthgwarra I once watched two males competing for the privilege of mating with a female. There was much writhing and entwining so that it was difficult to see where one snake ended and another began. Eventually one male conceded defeat and slithered off, leaving the others to it, as any gentleman would. I stayed to watch! After more twining and writhing the successful competitor slid along the full length of the female and, with both tails curled like hooks, the necessary bits came together and the job was done to their mutual satisfaction.

The males are more contrastingly marked than the females, the black zigzag along the back being bordered by a ground colour from white through brown and green. One that crossed my path near Bosigran was black and cinnamon, a very handsome creature. Adders emerge quite early if the weather is warm; mid-March is my personal earliest, and my latest recorded on 17 October 2001, when I saw one lying at the side of the path in the Cott Valley. It was very thin and I thought it dead, but just as I was about to pick it up, it slowly moved off into cover. I read later that they go into hibernation with an empty stomach.

Of grass snakes I can tell you very little. I have seen only one in many years of traipsing about the bogs, and that back in the late-1940s at Clodgy, St Ives. The compilers of the *Lizard Handbook* (1976) could find only one record for the area, although they mention two at Godrevy Cove in 1957. The Wildlife Information Service (WIS) of The Environmental Records Centre for Cornwall and the Isles of Scilly (ERCCIS) has recorded only some 75 sightings in Cornwall since 1980, so grass snakes are evidently quite rare here. They would be very reluctant, or foolish, to cross main roads so their distribution, like that of many terrestrial species, is likely to become fragmented.

Marazion beach is a favourite haunt of Brent geese when they arrive in October. They do not arrive every year, but it is probably the regenerating Zostera bed by the causeway that keeps them here when they do.

Slow-worms, which are sometimes reported as grass snakes, are much more widespread, and may be found throughout Cornwall hiding under stones in grassland, and may also be found beneath sheets of corrugated iron, an ideal hiding place for the beautifully striped young ones. They are somewhat nocturnal, although they do bask in the sun early in the year, putting themselves at risk from various predators. I have seen them caught by magpies, jackdaws, kestrels, buzzards and domestic cats. The ability to shed the tail as a distraction is common in all lizards, of which the slow-worm is a modified form, and I did once witness a magpie eat the shed tail while the slow-worm escaped into the vegetation. They, like true lizards, are often seen with but a black stump where a new tail is attempting to grow.

The common lizard is seen more frequently basking in the sun than the slow-worm, but they too are very wary, also being hunted by buzzards, kestrels and magpies, as well as being the main prey of the adder. They like vegetation that is not too thick, interspersed with rocks or a small area of matted vegetation where they may bask in the sun. Cornish stone 'hedges' are ideal. Lizards do not like your shadow falling on them, so keep your eyes ahead to increase the chances of finding one. The cleared margins along the coastal paths are favoured areas and the quiet observer is likely to have one come out and walk over his boots or backpack as he lies resting in the sun.

Gathering storms in autumn bring seabirds close to our shores. Many thousands can pass by in a single day at Pendeen, Gwennap Head (Porthgwarra) and here, at St Ives, where they also come into the bay for shelter and may be seen at close range.

Western or dwarf gorse Ulex gallii *is a distinct species flowering with the heathers in late summer and autumn, unlike its taller, ubiquitous relative, common gorse or furze* Ulex europaeus, *that can be found in flower throughout the year.*

The Penwith moors seem to go on for ever, but are, in fact, very fragmented, being only a fraction of their former extent.

Inset: *Among the less common migrants pausing on the moors and rough fields, may be found the occasional tawny pipit.*

Gurnard's Head. Fully exposed to westerly gales, this is a lichenologist's paradise. Every surface is coated in their growth, indicating pure, if somewhat turbulent, air.

This striated rock face near Bosigran, that the geologists among you will readily identify, is one of the very few substrates that are inhospitable to lichen and remain almost bare. Even here, there is an encrustation of very fine lichen that would require a specialist to identify.

Inset top: *The brilliant yellow of* Rhizocarpon geographicum. *This species is quite selective, preferring smoother rock faces in full sun, but despite this, is very widespread. I recognised it in New Zealand, Kazakhstan and Canada.*

Inset below: *The black* Verrucaria, *above its usual level, grows in competition with the grey-coating* Lecanoras *and* Ochrolechias.

When the bracken turns to burnished copper, we forgive its smothering green of summer. Cape Cornwall is a lookout for all the passing creatures of the sea, from birds to whales. A few puffins visit the offshore Brisons but apparently do not breed. A few remain on the islands of the north coast and possibly on Gull Rock in Veryan Bay.

In Zennor village black redstarts use the church tower as a fly-catching perch, while the willow scrub from the sea to Foage Farm is a favourite haunt of goldcrests and firecrests. On the coast there are said to be mermaids, but I have never seen one.

Gwennap Head is the most south-westerly point of the British mainland, and therefore the most distant; this could have been more appropriately named 'Land's End' than the other one. Bird-watchers from all over the world gather amongst the shelter of the rocks on the point during and after sou'westerly gales. Nearby Porthgwarra and its valley is a hotspot for finding rare birds from America and Asia.

The first black-headed gulls arrive in late summer and many more pass though in autumn, when they have lost the black colour of the head. The white leading edge of the wing is an identification feature.

Dotterel, so called because of their tame and trusting nature, may be too confiding for their own good, but their superb camouflage hides them from most people when they rest on our moors in autumn.

Mist-nets, so finely made as to be practically invisible in scrub, are deadly tools for catching birds when in the wrong hands. With training and strict adherence to rules that ensure the well-being of the birds, they are invaluable for bird-ringers. This, if you can see it, is one of my nets set in the valley at Porthgwarra nearly forty years ago.

A great tit hangs in a net. Skill and patience, together with good eyesight, is needed to extract the birds unharmed.

A pair of migrant blackcaps, caught in the same net. This is the species that has colonised west Cornwall as a breeder in the past fifty years. It is also found throughout in smaller numbers in winter, especially in gardens.

Some of our smallest birds, goldcrests and firecrests, are not easy to separate because of their quick movements and propensity for staying in thick cover, but a good look will reveal the startling white eye-stripe and golden shoulders of the latter. Look for them in autumn and winter at Helston Amenity Centre and in public gardens in towns.

Siskins, while much more common as a passage migrant flying over in October, are more often seen feeding on peanuts in Cornish gardens in late winter and in April, presumably when migrants from the Continent are moving north again.

A quiet winter's day on Loe Pool, Helston. Until the building of Drift, Stithians and Siblyback reservoirs this was the only large area of fresh water in Cornwall. It holds flocks of pochard, wigeon, teal, shoveler and tufted ducks.

Inset: *A male smew, always uncommon, and with hard winters becoming less frequent, not often seen in Cornwall. Those that are driven here by the cold are usually the duller females and immatures. However there was a fine male on Loe Pool in February 2002.*

Perched in typical pose on a prominent cliff-top rock, which is evidently used by many birds, a wheatear awaits a passing fly. The most widespread of all European birds, they breed occasionally on cliff-top slopes such as this and among stone walls on the high moors. They are the first passerine bird to arrive in spring, and among the last to leave.

Sunrise at St Ives, when early worms catch the birds. Fishermen and birders do best at dawn but high tide at any time will find divers, grebes and cormorants fishing in our harbours.

As migration gets underway, Cornish harbours are well worth checking for rare gulls after storms. At low tide several species of gull roost on the sandbanks, while maritime waders such as turnstones and purple sandpipers search the exposed seaweeds for invertebrates.

A well-known mining relic, the area of the Crowns Mine is also a superb spot for observing the passing seasons. Dolphins, porpoises and basking sharks are regularly seen here.

Puffballs at Pendarves.

Here are some cliff-top fungi making a fine autumn sight but which I have yet to identify. Some of them are quite difficult and it is still a comparatively new subject for most of us. On the Continent they eat far more than us and suffer more fatalities. So be careful!

The dreaded honey fungus that plays havoc with garden shrubs usually grows in clumps on the ground, but occasionally emerges further up the trunk.

Providing a feast that no bird can resist, Bentham's cornel is laden down with fruits in early autumn.

Redwings, usually birds of open fields, find berries of myrtle irresistible, as do all the thrushes. This one bush also had mistle thrushes, blackcaps, robins and firecrests, among others, feeding on it until the end of December, for the berries are protracted in ripening.

Marazion Marsh from the railway bridge. The RSPB is controlling willow scrub and opening up channels to improve the year-round habitat. Listen for Cetti's warblers in the nearby blackthorn.

It was at Marazion that I saw my first flock of little egrets after seeing them very rarely in ones and twos. They now spend the winter here in flocks of up to 20 or so, and make a fine sight against the autumn reeds.

Doe and young rabbit. The rabbit is the one wild mammal that everyone has seen, yet few people have any idea of its complex biology. The young are born in especially excavated chambers off the main warren and are weaned very quickly, soon becoming independent. They need to be very wary as they are staple diet of many predators and few survive to adulthood. A doe can produce ten young a year in two or three litters, the first of which can breed in the same season, before reaching adult size. Such potential for population explosion is naturally controlled by both predators and the females reabsorbing a high proportion of embryos before birth.

Kynance Cove on the Lizard is noted for its wild-flower community, and parties of visiting ornithologists enjoy both its birds and scenery in spring and autumn.

Trevaylor Wood in January. Beech woods, with their winter carpets of bronze and tracery of light green leaves in spring, are always a pleasure to visit. Autumn brings out the fungi and in such woods are found the colourful Russulas. Woodpeckers and nuthatches are easier to see on the bare trunks in winter. Come spring, the trees will echo with birdsong.

GWAF

WINTER

Out of the bosom of the air,
Out of the cloud-folds of her garment shaken,
Over the woodlands brown and bare,
Over the harvest-fields forsaken,
Silent, and soft, and slow
Descends the snow.

Snow Flakes H.W. Longfellow

With global warming, snow and ice are likely to become even more infrequent here and birds will spend their winters in the north, so we are told. But while waiting for those balmier days, we have plenty to see during the current mild winters in Cornwall. The short hours of daylight force birds into concentrated feeding activities, unless they are owls, whereas most mammals, being nocturnal, go about their business as usual. Very few hibernate in the true sense, although many will sleep through periods of bad weather. Even the cold-blooded reptiles and amphibians that are supposedly obliged to curtail their activities in severe winters are not dormant for long. I have found an active toad on 9 December, pairs coupled up for spawning in my garden on 30 January (2002) and you will certainly find frogspawn from the first week in January in most years, despite most of the really severe weather occurring later. The eggs are able to stand some freezing of the surface water but the old frogs must, presumably, retire to their dens again. Toads spawn later and are much more plentiful than frogs here, for they survive in dry conditions when not breeding whereas the frog requires damp marshes and bogs all year round. That is what the books say, but not all frogs have read the

Living at the bottom of a valley can be very difficult, even with a slight snowfall, if it freezes.

rules. In one Cornish town garden, completely walled and miles from any wet ground, the householder found ten adult frogs that lived in a neglected corner under a bit of old wood that had not been disturbed for many years. They may have been brought in as tadpoles of course and been unable to escape when mature. They certainly knew what to do in his garden pond when it was built, although the goldfish ate the tadpoles.

Newts, despite not being so frequently seen, are the most common amphibians in Cornwall. We have but one species, the palmate newt, and it is everywhere. They too emerge in late winter and colonise every garden pond, where the numbers can be astonishing. I was called to one garden where the lady had a phobia about them and wanted them cleared from the pond. When the pond, which was only about 2 x1 metres, was drained and the newts put in a bucket we had about 20 of them which we put in our pond. I was pretty sure that within a few days her pond would be recolonised to optimum numbers. But there is no point in scaring people and, if she introduced the planned goldfish, they would probably eat all the 'newt-poles' as well as all the dragonfly larvae, beetles, pond skaters, water-boatmen and all the other forms of life that should be there, and ensure that the water was never clear. Goldfish and wild pond-life do not mix.

It is during winter that our estuaries and reservoirs are at their most interesting. We are now fortunate in having several stretches of fresh water where formerly there were none. Prior to the formation of Loe Pool, itself a very recent phenomenon in geological terms, there was no sizeable lake or pool of fresh water anywhere in Cornwall. The small ones on the Lizard (Hayle Kimbro, Croft Pascoe and Ruan), together with Marazion Marsh, would have attracted nearly all of the few wildfowl that visited the area. Then came some small reservoirs, as at Crowan, and Bussow at St Ives, but it was not until the building of Drift, Siblyback and Stithians dams that the numbers of wintering freshwater ducks increased. The numbers are still quite low by national standards but all of the regular visitors to Britain and a good few rarities occur on them. They are great places to learn your wildfowl identification techniques but their real value is apparent in hard winters, when hundreds of weather-driven birds congregate there to await the passing of the freeze.

The estuaries, on the other hand, have always been there and have deteriorated rather than improved. The Hayle estuary must be the most long-suffering wildlife site in the world. For two hundred years industrial man has done his best to destroy it, and probably for many years before that, and it is still under threat. However, this is not the place to chronicle the past disasters that have encroached upon our estuaries with accelerating frequency, or the dangers facing them now. Let us enjoy what remains. There are days in even a normal winter when the estuaries are packed with birds. Hundreds of gulls, wigeon, teal, curlew and other waders, golden plover resting, shelduck, together with divers, grebes, egrets and kingfishers, congregate here, to the delight of an increasing number of people who appreciate them. There are no better places to become acquainted with such a diversity of bird-life in so small an area as on an estuary. There has been no shooting allowed on Hayle for fifty years, since the Cornwall Birdwatching Society bought the shooting rights as a protection strategy, and the birds know it, having become remarkably tame.

When I began regularly watching here in about 1950 the duck, being frequently shot at, were wild and wary and kept well out of shotgun range. Even now you can see newcomers in the sky wheeling and circling, attempting to alight, losing their nerve and flying off again, uncertain if it is safe to alight amongst so much traffic, trains, cars, boats, people and pylons. They see the old-timers who come year after year quietly feeding, and eventually fly down to join the resident flocks, so today you can see them and all their glorious colours with the naked eye. The biggest natural danger to the waders on the mud is from one of their own avian kind, the peregrine falcon, which may be seen over the estuary several times a day. These are often young ones and fairly unskilled in hunting but, nevertheless, they put all the birds up in a panic when they fly over, an obvious clue to their presence. Even the great black-backs are wary of peregrines, as are all the other gulls, waders and ducks.

Gulls are birds for specialists, as they are not considered of great interest by most people and some are quite difficult to identify, especially the young ones. I have seen 14 species of gull on the Hayle estuary and there are a couple more found only at sea. As a child, I knew of only two kinds of gull: ordinary gulls, later to be herring gulls, and 'policemen' gulls, the great black-backed gulls whose black mantles, together with their tendency to intervene in quarrels among the others earned them the epithet. It is interesting to note that the glaucous gull, the northern equivalent of the great black-backed is known as the 'burgomaster' in Holland and France, where it appears in winter. The herring gull has evolved essentially as a scavenger. Before becoming dependent on man it was probably nothing like as prolific; its food supply would have been intermittent, depending on flotsam and beached carcasses and plunder stolen from other species, while its breeding requirement of predator-free islets or inaccessible, yet wide, cliff ledges restricted its breeding sites. Old photographs of the herring fisheries, with thousands of fish exposed, show not a gull in sight, whereas today they would descend in hordes were the fish to be left uncovered. Where they nested on mainland cliffs they were often shot at purely as target practice, especially in the Second World War when there was a surfeit of .303 rifles in the country. The first ones to settle on town roofs found a predator-free site within easy reach of humans who would fill their bellies day after day in exchange for a few poses for their snapshots. Security and a regular supply of food – what more can a gull ask? They recognise from afar individual people who regularly feed them and will fly down to meet them as they approach among the thousands of tourists on the harbour front.

I remember an incident some time ago when I was ringing herring gulls to see if they wandered far from home; (they don't). After trying all manner of ways to catch them, from a huge drop-net on 12ft poles on Porthgwidden to baited clap-nets, I found the best way was to entice them to snatch a morsel of bacon rind held in the fingers and grab them around the neck as they flew past. This required a certain amount of manual dexterity that I assumed had long left me until recently required to repeat the procedure for a television programme. Cameras are guaranteed to draw the crowds, so it was with some apprehension that I leaned over the harbour railing in readiness. Sure enough, the birds began circling and, being virtually trained by now to take food from the hand, one tried to snatch the bacon and 'with the quickness of the hand deceiving the eye', I grabbed it and brought it to ground in front of the camera. I had forgotten how sharp their beaks are until it tried to take a chunk out of my arm. I was glad they cut that bit from the final version, along with the moment when the bird had the wind knocked out of it when grabbed.

When I was catching the original birds for ringing, one tourist, clad in thin white vest and shorts, saw me and asked if he could hold one to be photographed with in true tourist tradition. Warning him that the rear end was liable to produce something unsavoury, I passed the bird over, a big male, and the man kept the rear end pointed at me, which I thought a bit unreasonable but it meant that the beak was towards his chest. Now, if ever you get bitten, 'pecked' is hardly accurate, by a large gull, never try to pull it off, for their beaks are designed to rip flesh. You should push whichever part is in its grip further down its gullet, when it will release you in fear of getting choked. I should have told the man at the time but one can't remember everything.

Up on the high ground, hawthorns lean away from the wind, stunted and gnarled. They nevertheless survive for many years, providing the migrant thrushes with their first meal on making landfall.

While his wife was posing the picture the gull grabbed the man by the pectoral muscle and dug in deep. Blood spread all down his chest, soaking the vest, increasing in volume as he pulled the bird away. I don't know if the moment was caught on camera for posterity but after releasing the man with appropriate murmurings of sympathy, I was glad they didn't see me laughing as they went off.

Some years ago an aunt of mine in St Ives found a fledgling herring gull down in her back garden, not sufficiently developed to fly back to the roof tops. She decided to feed it until it became strong enough to fly off. Great mistake! Having learned to fly, it had also learned the source of free dinners, so it came back every day for more and my aunt was convinced that she was now obliged to feed it for ever. This entailed going out with its dinner and waiting for it to appear, as leaving the food there unattended would mean feeding all the gulls in the parish. My aunt devised a plan whereby she rang a small hand-bell when she fed the gull, which soon learned to associate ding-a-ling with dinner. The problem was that my aunt kept losing the bell, so she hung it on a string outside the back door. One day, while my aunt was having a quiet cup of tea, the ringing of the bell drew her to the back door, where the gull was impatiently shaking the bell in its beak, which she found highly amusing. I thought this bird had learned something from Pavlov's dogs but apparently it was Skinner's pigeons, the ones that learned to get food by pecking the correctly coloured buttons. Maybe, but I reckon that was one pretty smart herring gull. By what psychologists call operant conditioning, it had trained my aunt to respond to a bell! It kept this routine up for years, demanding to be fed on time, eventually rearing its own brood in a nest on the roof of the garden shed.

When the snow does lie thick and that cold easterly sweeps across our bays, it seems absurd to think that so many birds come to Cornwall for the winter. The only reason they are here in such conditions is that it is much worse further north. The weather-driven redwings, fieldfares, lapwings and wildfowl undertook their main migration in autumn, when they were powered up with layers of fat laid down in the time of plenty. The winter movements are forced upon them at a time when reserves are low, when they have already endured the privation of a cold spell in their normal range. They are like refugees, driven out in the face of death, with little reserve to sustain them on the journey. I was given some woodcock shot under such conditions and the poor things were just skin and bone. I reckon the lead in them weighed more than the meat. Few birds are killed by the cold, incidentally; it is the shortage of food, locked up in ice or under snow that sees them off. Even little goldcrests can survive so long as the leaves and crevices in bark are free of ice. The worst conditions are freezing snow or rain and that which we rarely see here in Cornwall, a freezing fog that coats the trees in icicles and rime. We have not seen a hard winter for some years at the time of writing and this is nowadays attributed to global warming. Yet, apart from a few slurries, I was seventeen years old before I saw snow. In 1947 I went into the youth club one January evening. 'It's snowing,' I said. 'Ah,' said the leader, 'you don't know what snow is down here. It'll be gone in an hour.' There was still snow on the ground, in the corners of fields and valleys where the sun had not reached, until May.

The casualties among wild birds were terrible and the populations took years to recover, especially of water-birds such as herons whose food was completely out of reach beneath the ice. After the first few weeks there were no more pathetic redwings, no more lapwings in town gardens desperately staring at the frozen lawn in the hope of some thawing worm or beetle; they were all dead. The last hard winter for birds was in 1985/6 when the redwings and lapwings perished and littered the ground even in the woods, as at St Loy, where the thaw revealed hundreds of corpses. Surveys undertaken following these disasters indicate that the toughest bird in Britain is the unobtrusive dunnock, whose habit of foraging for tiny morsels among the leaf litter enables it to survive where others perish. Even when visiting feeding tables, it will find the most minute crumbs after the more aggressive birds have left an apparently empty tray.

On those days of bitter winds, when the sky is dark with cloud and the water black with their reflected shadows, or when the shores are obscured in drizzle, Cornish bays would seem as places to flee from, rather than havens of refuge. Seen from the shore in these conditions, with the choppy seas curling before the winds, there is nothing to be seen alive on the water. Even the gulls are lost to view as their grey mantles blend into the mists of the dark easterlies. It is only when the wind falls calm, the surface becomes smooth and the winter sunshine illuminates the bays in crisp brilliance that the life in the sea becomes apparent. When seen like this from some vantage point, guillemots, razorbills, gannets, and sometimes a scoter or an eider duck, may be easily seen. Look for movements: the slight splash as shags leap clear to gain momentum in their plunge to the depths, the ripple remaining as the auks submerge, or the forward lunge of divers. Each species has its own particular way of submerging and can often be identified thus when too distant for other details to be seen.

Sometimes, in the quiet after winter storms, the bays seem full of birds but, of all the species which spend the winters here, perhaps the most interesting and the most vulnerable is that which was known as herring bird by the Kernewek, and great northern diver by the Sawson (English). They are big, nearly as big as a gannet on the water, and the first arrivals in October are sometimes in full summer plumage, a handsome black and white with a spangled mantle and an elegant collar of stripes. These early birds might be failed breeders which leave early, or it might indicate that the adults normally migrate before the soberly-coloured young, dark grey above, white below, which arrive in mid-November.

Despite their local name, and the coincidence of their synchronised arrival, it was not the herrings the herring birds came for. They do feed on smaller fish such as blennies and gobies, which they find among the rocks, but their main diet here is shore crabs, which they search for on the sandy beds of sheltered bays and bring to the surface to dismember before swallowing them, shells and all. I have never seen them eat anything else, but the small fish are swallowed under water. It is not known for certain where these birds come from. Two-hundred or so pairs are known to nest in Iceland but the great majority breed on the lakes of forest and tundra in Canada, where they are known as loons.

You are unlikely to see one off our steep cliffs, but they are found all along the shores of Mount's Bay from Mousehole to Kynance. They are also numerous in the Carrack Roads and Falmouth and Veryan bays, important wintering areas for divers and grebes. In the St Ives Bay there are rarely more than half a dozen wintering, with maybe a dozen in Mount's Bay, although numbers vary. They are best seen off Porthgwidden, around the Carracks off Porthminster Point and, in Mount's Bay, off the Battery Rocks or even in the harbours at high tide. Many more pass by on autumn migration but they do not fly much in winter. In late winter and early spring they moult all the primary feathers simultane-ously and become flightless until the new ones grow, in preparation for the long flight back to their northern lakes. It is during the flightless period that great northern divers are at their most vulnerable, although they seem to have few natural predators here. They move north in April to await the thawing of their breeding lakes, which might be under 4 feet of ice in January, making our bays seem quite a balmy place to spend the winter, after all.

December and January are also the months to look for fin whales. They come fairly close inshore and dedicated observers have seen them off Cape Cornwall, Gwennap Head and in the outer stretches of Mount's Bay for several years.

I have never seen one, so perhaps I should also begin looking out to sea in winter. Calm weather is essential for all cetacean watching, and it might take many hours before being rewarded by the telltale spout. That's all you'll see of the whales but dolphins can appear at any time to reward the patient watcher.

The Cornish expression 'wished as a winnard' refers to the redwing, but it must not be thought that all our visiting redwings are 'wished'. Far from it, they come every year and spend the winter, together with fieldfares and golden plover, on the high fields, where most people never see them. Our normal winters are more wet than cold, with westerly winds keeping the temperatures above freezing. The birds arrive, survive, go off to breed and return, bringing their young ones with them, so the wintering population builds up. Or so it might be thought without considering the hazards of the migration itself, during which the weak succumb. So why fly all that way for nothing when the winters are mild? The danger is that in a succession of mild winters the urge to migrate to the extreme becomes less and the instinct weakens. When a hard winter comes, as it surely will, thousands of birds will be caught out and perish through being too far north, as has happened many times before, I am certain, and only the traditionalists and the strong will survive.

A recent phenomenon has been the increase in wintering warblers that normally go off to the Mediterranean or Africa. Chiffchaffs are as numerous around the amenity area at Helston in winter as they are in summer. They have learned to exploit the insects over the settlement tanks of the sewage works. In autumn they are joined by firecrests and, almost annually, by a yellow-browed warbler from Asia. The firecrests spend the winter here in this mild corner, as they do in the gardens of Penzance where in recent years they seem more common in winter than the resident goldcrests. That discreet populations within a species range develop their own migratory patterns might not be obvious, but they do. All the starlings wintering here come from the same breeding area, and all our summer visitors go off to winter in equally restricted areas in the south. The anomaly in this pattern is found in the black-cap populations. A fairly recent coloniser of west Cornwall, largely owing to the increase in woodland and scrub, blackcaps are now found breeding throughout and their delightful song may be heard in any wood. They are fairly short-distance migrants, wintering around the Mediterranean basin.

Our breeding birds come in spring and go by late August then, apart from the occasional lost migrant, there is a dearth. Late October sees the arrival of another small wave of immigrants, this time the winter visitors that stay with us until early March. You are more likely to see a blackcap in winter than in spring and summer, when they spend their time hidden in vegetation. The wintering birds begin to sing in February but are all gone before the summer migrants arrive from the south. It is thought that these wintering blackcaps are from Germany and eastern Europe and it seems incredible that our breeding population undertakes the risky migration only to be replaced by birds breeding nearer the Mediterranean than ours do. The wintering blackcaps are far fewer, of course, although steadily increasing, and most seem to prefer urban gardens and low scrub along watercourses. The only advantage for them seems to be in the slightly less hazardous migration, but a hard winter will undoubtedly catch them out and reverse the trend.

Most of these small winter visitors are found in gardens and regular feeding will encourage and sustain them through the cold spells, while planting suitable shrubs can improve what is a very large and important percentage of the environment utilised by wildlife. On those winter days when it might be too cold and wet to venture far into the countryside, it is very rewarding to watch the inhabitants of the countryside come to us. Even a net of peanuts outside an urban window will have its regular visitors. Small gardens and public parks alike are vital for many species now. For my part, I see more birds per metre in my town garden than I do in the countryside, and the small pond (no goldfish) is visited by all and sundry.

Of all the species coming and going with the seasons, none spend the summer in our gardens, yet in the winter there are several. This is probably because summer migrants are all insectivorous, while winter visitors are more likely to feed on nuts and seeds. Blackcaps feed mainly on berries in autumn, but what sustains them in winter I don't know. Chiffchaffs, goldcrests and firecrests feed on the tiniest of midges which seem to fly all year. Some species, blue tits being the most often observed, move on to mahonia in December and January when they may be seen sipping the sweet nectar from the yellow flowers.

While writing this chapter in January 2002 I heard a commotion from the birds in the garden. Looking out, I was delighted to see a male sparrowhawk standing up to its breast in our pond, about 10 metres away. Thinking it was about to have a bath, I remained still and watched. It stood there for some five minutes, all the while looking warily around while nearby magpies and jackdaws chattered their alarms, and I retreated further from the window glass each

Bird photography, even more than other forms of wildlife photography, can be fraught. Greenfinches on peanut-feeders are among the easiest, but even these take a degree of patience not found in many of us. A wildlife photographer friend claims to be the only person who fires an Aga on rejected 35mm transparencies. I sympathise with him after trying to get a few bird portraits for this book.

time it looked away. It eventually flapped to the edge of the pond, to my astonishment dragging with one talon a dead starling. Presumably, it had been caught immediately over the pond and both came down into the water.

The hawk stood over it while still looking warily about. Deciding there was a better dining room elsewhere, the edge of the pond being just about a metre from the boundary wall, it attempted to fly but the saturated feathers of the starling were evidently too heavy to carry, its own plumage also being completely soaked. It managed merely to flap a bit further away from the edge, still looking about with those intense red eyes. When finally satisfied that all was safe it proceeded to pluck the starling, beginning with the head. When the skull was fully exposed it ate the brain, taking very small bits at a time. Then it turned its attention to the body, ripping off the feathers of the breast. At this point one of the magpies attempted to steal the prey, but, despite being larger, was too wary to approach within striking distance of those talons. It sidled up with wings and tail spread, to make itself appear even larger I thought, and approached side-on, posturing with the tail fully spread and pointed at the hawk. It came within about 40 cms, dancing about in front of the hawk but, after a few minutes, seeing that it was not to be put off, the magpie flew to the top of the wall. The hawk then continued with plucking the starling, pausing

The piercing yellow eyes of this young male sparrowhawk, trapped for ringing at Porthgwarra, will change to red as it matures. The eyes of hawks, and most other birds, are exceptionally large, almost filling the skull, so tightly that they can barely move. I read that the pupils are slower to respond to changes in light than ours but, especially in birds of prey, because of the higher number of rods than cones in the retina, their visual acuity is eight time better. As it was once put to me, they can look at the stars and detect the movement of the constellations revolving around Polaris.

frequently to check for danger, looking around and listening to noises from nearby gardens. When it began eating in earnest I went for my camera, crawling about on the floor, so as not to be seen. I set it up and took several shots but with poor light and shooting at one-eighth of a second through the window glass, had little hope of success. The magpie made a second, half-hearted, attempt to steal the starling but soon flew off. The prey was finally eaten and the sparrowhawk flew off with a bulging crop. I inspected the remains and the body had been picked completely clean except for some muscle tissue on the thighs. The whole episode took just an hour, during which I marvelled at the amazing skill of these predators both in capturing and dismembering their prey. It took as much care as a master butcher in preparing its dinner, with those incredibly keen eyes continually on the watch. One does not have to travel miles to observe nature close at hand.

Crisp winter days invite us out for walks. The low sun is short-lasting, so get out early. This is the time to look for the open-country specialists that prey on the voles and mice in the dry grasses of moor and overgrown field. Of all our birds of prey, none is more evocative of fine cold days in mid-winter than the hen harrier. If ever a bird was badly named, this is it, for it is doubtful that it ever kill hens. That hen harriers take a few expensive grouse chicks on the northern moors cannot be disputed but in Cornwall they are of no harm to anybody. For a buzzard-sized bird with such a long wingspan they are quite delicate, frail even, and seem at the mercy of every breeze as they glide over the ground on wings held in a shallow V. They take small birds and mammals and I am always amazed that they can do so, for the slow, languid flight belies their dexterity when hunting. The long legs are their weapons, with sharp talons that flash out and grab any unsuspecting pipit flushed from cover. Though it seems the females are more often seen, that may not be accurate. Birds in that plumage are most often seen, but as females and young males are indistinguishable in the field, it is impossible to know the sex of these 'ringtails' as those in brown plumage are called. The adult males are very different. They are a delicate dove-grey with black wingtips and a white rump, and are truly handsome.

I wish I could tell you where to go to see one of these birds, which are a delight to watch but, alas, I cannot as they are as elusive as piskies. You might see one on the Bodmin or Penwith moors, or Nancekuke or over farmland. They are far-ranging and do not hold individual territories, all the birds in an area even coming together to roost, so one travels in hope, keeping one's eyes toward the distant horizon or valley bottom.

This photo taken through the window, is of a male sparrow-hawk that caught and ate a starling by the pond in our garden. The red under-parts indicate a male and the red eyes an adult.

In looking for the hen harrier, you are as likely to see a short-eared owl. Of all our owls, these are the ones you are most likely to see in daylight in winter. They inhabit the same open country as harriers but are more common. They occur almost annually on the same downs and moors, occasionally in small groups, and begin hunting during the late afternoon, or at any time of day if hungry. They hunt over stretches of country where long moor grass or overgrown fields harbour voles and mice. Unlike the harriers, once established on a winter territory, they tend to stay there while the food lasts, so having found one you can go back time and again to watch them in their silent flight as they quarter the ground like gigantic moths.

Ravens begin building or repairing their nests in January and lay eggs in March. Hard winters suit them, for they clean up the carcases of birds killed off in the cold. Even the wren wastes no time in winter and the cocks will be building in suitable weather, which is not, as you might think, when the sun is shining. On 19 February I saw one wren nest-building in ivy on a garden wall in pouring rain. Not so daft as might be thought. In wet conditions the leaves and grasses with which they build are damp and pliable, easily worked into shape in the progressing dome. When they dry out they form a stiff yet flexible nest. This particular nest was evidently to the hen's liking and the pair continued building intermittently until mid-April. Two eggs were laid but the pair abandoned nest and eggs, perhaps because of a cat that favoured sitting on the wall above. Two months is a long time for small birds to spend nest-building and most, especially summer visitors for whom time is 'of the essence', take only a few days.

No account of wildlife in Cornwall, at whatever season, would be complete without some mention of our national bird. The catalogue of losses from the birds of Cornwall makes depressing reading. Within living memory we have lost the partridge, the quail, the cirl bunting, and we can no longer hear the call of the corncrake or the delightful song of the woodlark. Even the humble house sparrow is in decline. All these have succumbed to the degradation of their habitat through changes in agriculture. Others have gone for reasons which are unexplained and the saddest loss of all was that of our beloved Cornish chough. It is now over half a century since they bred in 1947, although a pair lived together without breeding until 1967. After the death of its partner the last bird survived for six lonely years and finally died in 1973.

Why they went remains a matter of some conjecture. They seem never to have been directly persecuted as pests, but were taken from the nest as pets and a stuffed chough in a glass case was a prized possession, to be displayed along with the stuffed peregrine falcon. Throughout most of its wide range, which extends from the west of Ireland to the coast of China on the Yellow Sea, it is a bird of mountains, up to 3600 metres in the Soviet Union, and our birds were something of an anomaly, breeding as they did at sea level. They forage among alpine meadows and scree, searching for insects among the stones, which is why they were at home in working slate quarries in central Wales and on the spoil from our own tin mines.

The loss of the British sheep flock in the wake of cheaper imports of lamb from Australia and New Zealand no doubt contributed to the decline here, for choughs also like to forage among short turf, which is soon overgrown with scrub when there are no grazing animals to keep it down. There were other factors affecting them, however, and the decline was not restricted to the UK, where they were formerly common and widespread on all coasts. Disastrous declines have been recorded throughout Western Europe, with severe losses to the point of extinction in France, Switzerland and Austria. Changes in agriculture seem unlikely to have affected birds living at such high altitudes. The question of disease must also be considered. A worldwide epidemic would have gone undiagnosed two hundred years ago when the decline began and, while there was normally some movement of individuals between the sedentary colonies, any serious decline would necessarily be followed by inbreeding, further weakening already vulnerable, isolated populations.

There is no doubt that egg collectors hastened the end, the eggs of Cornish choughs being highly prized and all the more so as they became rarer, such is the mentality of collectors. Whatever the cause, they disappeared, apparently extinct. For those of us who can remember seeing them performing their aerial acrobatics about the Cornish cliffs, with their glossy plumage, brilliant red bills and legs, and haunting calls, it was a sad loss indeed. The name 'chough' is considered onomatopoeic, but to me they don't say anything like 'chuff', more of a 'chough', to rhyme with bough (as on the trees), and I once met an old Cornish man who did indeed call them 'chows'. The Latin name, *Pyrrhocorax*, fire crow, is from the myth that they carried fire in their bills. The proper Cornish name is palores, the digger, shoveller, or navvy, from 'pal', a shovel, and 'palas', to dig, though why it should be the female form of the word is a mystery. They were also known, according to R. Morton Nance, as 'chogha gar ruth', red-legged jackdaw. Of all the crows, they are the most benign, having no predatory designs on other species, unlike their cousins the carrion crow, raven and magpie. The plans to reintroduce them are well known, with breeding programmes undertaken with several captive pairs, while the National Trust have been using sheep and cattle to clear scrub from clifftops in preparation for their release. So far, however, those birds that laid eggs usually failed to rear any young and it has not yet led to any releases.

It seemed they were gone for ever, when early in 2001, three turned up of their own volition on a favoured cliff. They proved to be a pair, a true male and female pair, and an unmated singleton, and there were unconfirmed reports of others being seen elsewhere. As yet, until DNA tests have been done, their origin is unknown. It is possible that someone decided to bypass regulations and bring them in unofficially, but more likely that they were driven from Ireland or Brittany, or even Spain, by strong offshore winds. Having made it to Cornwall they set up home at a time when the cliffs were deserted by humans because of foot and mouth restrictions. Whatever the circumstances, it was the most exciting event in our ornithology for many years, and the birds could be seen living up to their Cornish appellation by digging into ant's nests and amongst the thrift for beetles or whatever they could find.

There was apprehension that they might not survive the winter but they came through it successfully and, in the spring of 2002, found a cave and built a nest. A twenty-four hour guard was set to watch over them by a dedicated band of volunteers, to whom we are all grateful and without whose vigilance a couple of brain-dead egg collectors would have robbed the nest. It was in unsprayed fields that they found sustenance to support the brood, and when I visited the site in early May they were making regular visits to the nest and by the second week it was confirmed that they had four young, one of which was later lost. Before they fledged the three survivors were examined and sexed as all male. This might have been considered a disappointment but it will prevent inbreeding should any stray females arrive. At the time of writing the family had moved away from the breeding site and there are rumours of another pair outside our area. Let's hope that further breeding will follow although they have to face many dangers before a viable population of our beloved choughs becomes established. Yet, if these birds came, it is not impossible that others will follow, so it is worth looking for them and listening for their echoing calls on our cliffs. Their return is as a sign, an omen of hope, that our wild things will survive, despite our mistreatment of them, and continue to delight us and future generations with their presence.

Winter on the high moors can be bleak but beautiful. Watch Croft is the highest point of west Cornwall at 252 metres.

Hundreds of wigeon winter on our estuaries. They feed on the green weed lying on the mud, carrying it in full beaks to the water and carefully washing it before eating it. You can see them waddling back and forth in little groups when the tide is out. At high tide they gather in flocks and rest.

Hardy ponies do well on the moors while the weather stays open, and their hooves help keep bracken under control.

Ding Dong Mine. Perhaps because of its name, this is one of the most well-known mines in Cornwall. In the distance is Greenborough Mine, higher and more prominent in the landscape and often confused with Ding Dong. Barn owls, kestrels, jackdaws and crows all use these old ruins for nesting so long as there is not too much disturbance.

Gorse in December provides a soft yet vibrant contrast to these ruins at Kenidjack Castle.

Dark skies on a northerly threaten snow over Godrevy. The island holds colonies of shags and herring gulls, and a few razorbills on the seaward side make tentative visits in late winter prior to breeding. Dolphins may be seen moving through the inner sound and grey seals breed in the nearby caves and coves.

Lanyon Quoit, with Carn Galver to the left and Greenborough Mine to the right. This is right in the middle of good wintertime bird-watching country, with flights of golden plover, lapwing and the occasional short-eared owl on offer.

The stone monuments have more atmosphere of their ancient past in winter. The Nine Maidens (Naw Meyn – nine stones) reflect the cold sky in a wet winter. While they remain unfrozen, these pools are used by passing birds for bathing and drinking.

What is this? It seems to have a hole in it. I have seen a few hen harriers and short-eared owls from here. Meyn-an-Tol is always worth a visit at any time of year but tends to be a bit crowded in summer. Crawling through the hole is said to cure rickets but gives you backache for the rest of your days.

Recently acquired by the Cornwall Wildlife Trust, the disused clay-pit at Georgia has great potential as a wildlife refuge. This is another example, of which we have so many, of wildlife reclaiming old industrial sites, in this case over about a hundred years. With a little encouragement the process is much quicker.

Hayle estuary has seen many changes since I began watching here in the 1940s. This old picture shows the chimneys of the power station, and the part of the river in the foreground is now covered by the widened road. On the Lelant side, where grey mullet spawned and kingfishers and wood sandpipers fed, we lost a salt-marsh under a municipal rubbish tip, which is now leaching toxic effluent into the mud.

With the vegetation dying off, more persistent fungus is revealed. Here a fungus and a lichen make a startling combination growing on dead gorse. Both play an important part in the breakdown and recycling of all living tissue.

Wildlife can be studied wherever you go, especially if you take it with you. This colony of lichen has travelled hundreds of miles. Friends who owned the car were disconcerted one day to realise that they were being pursued by a strange man in another vehicle. Despite travelling through convoluted country lanes he was still on their tail when they reached home, whereupon they discovered he was from the British Lichen Society and was anxious to examine their car. He identified 27 lichen species, including three very rare ones, and one never recorded in the UK before.

The area known as Ryan's field, at Hayle estuary, as it was before being taken over by the RSPB.
At high tide terns and waders may be viewed from the new hide.

The teal is the smallest of our wild duck and one of the most common to winter here, both on estuaries and fresh water.

Inset left: *Turnstones visit the estuary, but are more at home on pebbly beaches where invertebrates are hiding under stones.*

Inset right: *An old friend to many visitors to Copperhouse Creek, this ring-billed gull first arrived from Canada as a yearling and has returned to the same spot for many years, developing a taste for saffron buns and the ends of pasties. It probably spends the summers in Sweden where one is recorded every year when our bird is absent.*

Little egrets are now common on all our Cornish estuaries, and a beautiful addition to our bird-life.

Always a fine sight, swan numbers stay fairly constant. They gather together after breeding to spend the winter in the estuary.

Drift Reservoir, not the most photogenic location but its shores are an important site for wintering wildfowl and breeding passerines.

Inset: *A flotilla of mute swans, with tufted duck behind them. As many as 40 swans spend the winter here, having learned that they get well fed by nearby residents.*

Polypody ferns cover a dead tree trunk at Godolphin Woods. Overly tidy forestry, with all the dead wood cleared away, results in a less interesting woodland with fewer fungi and ferns, and no nesting cavities for birds.

The delightful grey wagtail is one of my favourite birds. They formerly bred on all of our streams but are now far less common, for reasons which are unknown. As winter visitors, they are widespread and visit garden ponds searching for aquatic insects.

Regular feeding will encourage birds to return daily. Starlings are now decreasing. Whereas there were over 20 visiting our feeding station five years ago, in the winter of 2002/3 there were just four or five.

This page and opposite: *These old photos of Marazion Marsh in the 1960s illustrate the more extensive open water of those days. The reed beds are of fairly recent growth and show the gradual transition from open pools through reeds to scrub, and eventually dry land. Such sites need intensive management to retain their character.*

This area is now covered by reeds and scrub, resulting in a change in the birds visiting the marsh. There are more breeding reed warblers and more wintering bitterns, though still rare, and far fewer waders. Migrant hobbies sometime stop here in autumn to feed on dragonflies.

Starlings at Marazion Marsh are a spectacular sight that may not last much longer if the present rate of decline continues.

Winter rain fills the streams, as here at Nanquidno, and dippers move from higher levels right down to the coast.

Porth Nanven at the bottom of Cott Valley; this raised beach tells a story of geological changes over millennia. The round boulders were shaped when they were below sea level. The raised beach also shows itself at Nanquidno and to a lesser extent at other places around the coast.

Wild weather brings its own beauty to Porthcurnow, with Treryn Dynas cliff castle and the Logan rock in the distance.

Leach Pottery, with Barbara Hepworth's 'Crucifixion' all frozen up, in 1963, one of the hardest winters since 1947 which was the worst of the century. In both, dead birds were lying in the streets as well as the countryside, starved and frozen stiff.

POSTSCRIPT

In this quick journey through the seasons we have merely touched upon all that is to be seen and enjoyed out there in the open air. More has been omitted than included in my reminiscences, for it would take several books to cover everything. Come out and see it and, wherever we go, whatever we see, we cannot but marvel at the complexity, the beauty, the intricacy, of life around us out there in Cornwall. Whether at the resurgence of spring, the exuberance of summer, the autumnal fulfilment, or in the dead of winter when bare twigs are 'dormant', our wildlife offers an abiding interest and excitement for those who wish to share it. The sights and sounds of high summer are ever enchanting, but, even on the coldest, dullest days, all is eagerly preparing for the annual resurgence. Deep inside those dry buds the embryonic leaves and flowers that produce the aromas of summer and fruits of autumn are already forming, in some cases are already formed, for dormant is a concept of ours, not of nature, which is ever vibrant. Spring is on the way, always.

N.R.P. Penzance 2002

Only on our three larger rivers, the Fal, Fowey and Camel, can such scenes as this be seen, but they serve to emphasise the great diversity of habitat to be found in Cornwall. This quiet stretch of the River Camel, near Polbrock, is the haunt of dippers, kingfishers, grey wagtails and otters. Daubenton's bats may sometimes be seen flitting over these open reaches in broad daylight.

The very end. I hope you enjoyed it.

RECOMMENDED READING

There are excellent books on every aspect of British Wildlife but for first-class grounding information not found in most guides I recommend Collins' *New Generation* Guides. I am particularly indebted to those who have produced the literature that enabled me to enjoy the Cornish countryside to the full. Obviously, I have not read everything on the subject but I recommend the following among the many good things available.

Bird Life in Cornwall. B.H. Ryves. Collins, 1948. A classic, long out of print but occasionally available in second-hand bookshops.

The Birds of Cornwall and the Isles of Scilly. R.D. Penhallurick, Headland, 1978.*

The Butterflies of Cornwall. Penhallurick.

A Natural History of Land's End. Jean Lawman. Tabb House, 2002. An excellent introduction to the wildlife of the peninsula, with detailed information on what to see and where.

The Nature of Cornwall. Bere, Blamey & Coombs. Barracuda Books with Cornwall Naturalists' Trust (now Cornwall Wildlife Trust). Limited edition, 1982.*

A Handbook of the Natural History of The Lizard Peninsula. Turk & Turk. University of Exeter, 1976.*

The Grey Seals of the West Country. By Stephen Westcott. Westcott in co-operation with CWT 1996.* A first-class study of our largest breeding mammal.

Wild Cornwall, and other periodic publications of Cornwall Wildlife Trust.

Ydhyn yn Kernow, Birds in Cornwall. The Annual Reports of the Cornwall Bird-watching Society.

Other recommended guides include:

BIRDS
Collins Bird Guide. Mullarney, Svensson, Zettersrom & Grant. Collins, 1999.

The Birds of Europe. Lars Jonsson. Helm, 1992.

British Birds of Prey. Leslie Brown, Collins New Naturalist, 1976.*

REPTILES
The British Amphibians and Reptiles. M. Smith. Collins New Naturalist, 1951.*

INSECTS
A Field Guide to the Insects of Britain and Northern Europe. Michael Chinery. Collins, 1973.*

The Butterflies of Britain and Europe. Higgins & Hargreaves. Collins, 1983.

The Dragonflies of Great Britain and Ireland. Hammond, revised Merritt. Harley, 1983.

MAMMALS
A Field Guide to the Mammals of Britain and Europe. Van Den Brink. Collins, 1967 *

MARINE LIFE
Sea Shore of Britain and Europe. Hayward, Smith & Shields. Collins, 1996

A Handguide to the Sea Coast. Ovenden & Barrett. Treasure Press, 1987.*
(A little gem of a book, worth ten times the price)

The Sea Shore. C.N. Young. Collins New Naturalist, 1949.*

(* If you can get them)